Beautiful Button Jewelry

By Susan Davis

Beautiful Button Jewelry

By Susan Davis

Sterling Publishing Co., Inc., New York

A Red Lips 4 Courage Book
Red Lips 4 Courage Communications, Inc.
8502 E. Chapman Ave., 303
Orange, CA 92869
Web site: www.redlips4courage.com

Every effort has been made to ensure that all information in this book is accurate. However, due to differing conditions, tools, and individual skills, the publisher cannot be responsible for any injuries, losses, and/or other damages, which may result from the use of the information in this book.

This volume is meant to stimulate decorating ideas. If readers are unfamiliar or not proficient in a skill necessary to attempt a project, we urge that they refer to an instructional book specifically addressing the required technique.

Library of Congress Cataloging-in-Publication Data

Davis, Sue, 1946-
  Beautiful button jewelry / Susan Davis.
      p. cm.
  Includes bibliographical references and index.
  ISBN-13: 978-1-4027-2644-6
  ISBN-10: 1-4027-2644-9
  1. Jewelry making. 2. Button craft. I. Title.

TT212.D425 2005
745.594'2--dc22
                                        2005027793

10 9 8 7 6 5 4 3 2
Published by Sterling Publishing Co., Inc.
387 Park Avenue South, New York, NY 10016
©2005 by Susan Davis
Distributed in Canada by Sterling Publishing
c/o Canadian Manda Group, 165 Dufferin St.
Toronto, Ontario, Canada M6K 3H6
Distributed in the United Kingdom by GMC Distribution Services,
Castle Place, 166 High Street, Lewes, East Sussex, England BN7 1XU
Distributed in Australia by Capricorn Link (Australia) Pty. Ltd.
P.O. Box 704, Windsor, NSW 2756, Australia
Printed and Bound in China
All Rights Reserved

Sterling ISBN-13: 978-1-4027-2644-6
        ISBN-10: 1-4027-2644-9

For information about custom editions, special sales, premium and corporate purchases, please contact Sterling Special Sales Department at (800) 805-5489; or e-mail specialsales@sterlingpub.com.

A Family's Passion

One summer afternoon
in 1960, a small girl sat high on her mother's old mahogany bed, carefully sorting the contents of the button tin marked Cigars 5 Cents into piles by size, color, material, and shape. As she sorted her treasures, taking special care with her favorite deep red celluloid apples and iridescent rhinestone "diamonds," her mother pressed the peddle of the Singer sewing machine again and again, humming as she turned crisp prints into new school dresses for her three teenage daughters.

It was a companionable time for the busy mother and her smallest daughter, a welcome respite in the hectic household. The mother, glancing at her absorbed daughter, commented, "You know, Susan, good buttons always make the outfit. Nothing cheapens a dress like inferior buttons."

Twenty-five years later, the youngest daughter, now 30, returned to her small hometown after college and early career years in the city. She and her husband built a farmhouse and started a small gourmet vegetable business. She loved taking time in the afternoons to visit with her grandmother, who at 95 still

Left: This yellow cigar tin from the 1940s was the button tin of my childhood. It resided next to my mother's sewing machine, in a mahogany armoire she used as a sewing cabinet, nestled among shoe boxes of paper patterns and stacks and stacks of fabric scraps.

presided over a half-acre flower garden and a house layered with an almost geologic accumulation of possessions from her nine decades of life.

One particular afternoon they explored the contents of a bottom dresser drawer together, the granddaughter pulling out artifacts and the grandmother reminiscing about their origins and meaning. First came a rose gold Victorian locket with a favorite aunt's picture inside; then a velvet jewelry case with a sparkling crystal choker and "ear bobs," a gift from her husband; and at last, dozens of small boxes of buttons. Candy boxes, cough drop boxes, and stationery boxes, all filled with buttons of every description, every button that ever crossed the path of this woman who was born

during Reconstruction and who raised a family during the Depression and who, by golly, was never going to throw anything useful away!

The youngest daughter was of course me, and on that afternoon with my grandmother an idea lept into my mind (you could have almost seen the cartoon light bulb above my head) that changed the course of my life. Holding up a pair of sparkling jet glass buttons from the 1930s, I said, "Grandma, these buttons would make great earrings." She, who recycled everything from plastic bags to coffee tins before it was stylish to do so, said, "Well, honey, yes they would!" and cheerfully donated her boxes of buttons to my new cause (the cause of adding to our meager farming income).

Several trips to the hardware and crafts stores and a few weeks later, I offered my first button earrings for sale on a card table at a local crafts fair. Shoppers were puzzled, then intrigued. Though I later discovered that turning buttons into earrings had been a common hobby during the Depression, it seemed an ingenious and completely new idea on that day. By the show's end I had almost sold out.

Left: My maternal grandmother, Leola Goodman Scales. Born in Illinois in 1892, she came to New Orleans in the 1920s. She kept her buttons in this Whitman's Sampler candy box.

Top: This is Bettie Gandy Garrett, my paternal grandmother, who at age 95 helped inspire me to begin making jewelry from buttons. Born in 1889, a child of Reconstruction and a woman of the Depression, she saved everything possible, including some 30 boxes of buttons.

Above: Published in the 1940s, The Button String *tells the story of button charm strings. During the late 19th and early 20th centuries, young women saved buttons, stringing them on long cords until they had 999 buttons. When the 1000th button was placed on the string, the young lady's Prince Charming would appear.*

Thus was born Grandmother's Buttons more than two decades ago. From that small card table our business has grown into a jewelry company with wares sold in more than a thousand shops and boutiques in all 50 United States as well as Canada. My husband, Donny Davis, joined me in the company in 1988, after torrential rains (even by Louisiana standards) destroyed his entire

crop one June. We have truly enjoyed working together through all of our business ups and downs—his much higher-level math and business skills complementing my drive and creativity.

In 1994 we purchased our historic town's original bank building in St. Francisville, Louisiana, an imposing neo-Romanesque brick structure that dates from 1905. We opened our retail store in the bank's lobby in 1995, using the 16-foot ceilings, mosaic tile floor, and original oak woodwork as a dramatic setting for the cases of jewelry and eclectic books, gifts, accessories, and Victoriana we offered. Just a few months

Above Left: Our town's old bank building is now the home of Grandmother's Buttons.

Above: The bank's vault is home to our button museum and our precious treasures—rare and one-of-a-kind buttons.

Left: Now my customers walk on this floor, but its mosaic tiles loom large in my earliest memories. As a young girl, I was always so intimidated by the lofty ceilings and overall grandeur of our local bank building that I kept my eyes trained on the mosaic tiles while my parents did their banking.

later we transformed the old bank vault into a tiny 10-foot-square museum of antique buttons—certainly one of the smallest and most uniquely placed museums in the country. An immediate hit that has been featured in *Victoria, Country Home, Southern Living* and *Southern Accents* magazines, our museum features eight cases of mounted buttons, one from the 18th century, five from the 19th century, and two from the 20th century.

I often wonder what my grandmother would make of the strange and exciting places her 30-odd boxes of buttons have taken me. Though she lived for three more years after the start of our company, her mind was clear for only a few months after Grandmother's Buttons, named in her honor, was born. So it has been a source of great joy to me that my mother, now in her late 80s, has been able to watch and participate in our growth and accomplishments.

An artistic and resourceful woman, my mother has delighted in the adventures on which buttons have taken me: spelunking for vintage caches in dark and dusty basements in New York's Garment District; visiting the modest brick home of a button collector whose personal collection is worth almost a million dollars; overcoming my terror of appearing before a national audience on QVC television shopping program; exploring the flea markets of Shanghai in search of the perfect beads to complement our buttons; and working behind the scenes with some of the finest museums in the country to create custom pieces.

As a business associate of my father's once asked in amazement, if not dismay: "Who would have thought she could have done all of this with just some buttons?"

Of course the secret here is that these were not "just some buttons." Rather they were, and are, very special and historic buttons indeed.

Susan Davis

Above: A summer-time necklace of jade, glass, and bone beads, centered with one mother-of-pearl button, just one of the many sold in our retail store and catalog.

Bottom Left: Rhinestone brooches featuring antique button centers are a popular item in our store.

Left: Each display case in the museum houses buttons from different historical times.

Contents

Foreword . . . . Page 6

Introduction . . . . Page 12

Chapter 1 Getting Started . . . . Page 16

Chapter 2 Victorian Metal Buttons . . . . Page 26

Chapter 3 Victorian Jet Glass Buttons . . . . Page 70

Chapter 4 Antique Mother-of-Pearl Buttons . . . . Page 76

Chapter 5 Antique Porcelain & China Buttons . . . . Page 92

Chapter 6 Modern Glass Buttons . . . . Page 106

Chapter 7 Bakelite & Celluloid Buttons . . . . Page 116

About the Author . . . . Page 140

Where To Find It . . . . Page 141

Index . . . . Page 142

Bibliography . . . . Page 143

History of the Button

When I began my hunt for antique buttons to transform into jewelry, I combed flea markets and antique stores (1985 was well before the advent of eBay) for duplicates of the much used and loved buttons I had found in my grandmother's many tins and boxes: tiny pearls from generations of baby clothes; a few Victorian brass and jet glass buttons from my great-grandmother's dresses; and sparkling rhinestone and luster glass buttons from those special suits and evening gowns of the 1930s and '40s. To me, these comprised the world of antique buttons.

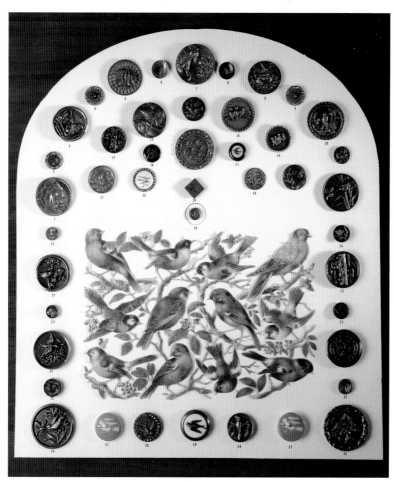

Imagine my shock, then, when I discovered that the humble button had a past far grander than anything I had imagined. The plain, four-hole disk that has become an icon of sorts for simpler, more homespun times has certainly existed for centuries, but alongside it were many glorious cousins: buttons of gold and precious gems, hand-painted ivory, micro-mosaics, and champlevé enamel—indeed, buttons made of everything from tortoise shell to butterfly wings, sapphires to Sevres porcelain.

Though in our business and throughout this book I do not use extremely rare and valuable buttons made prior to 1850, I think it is worth telling their story. Buttons through the centuries have functioned as tiny windows into the art, craft, history, legend, and even the politics of the day. Seeing the myriad forms they have taken and roles they have played can only make us appreciate the Victorian, Edwardian, and Art Deco buttons that we do use all the more.

The origins of the button are shrouded in mystery. Archeologists have discovered button-like objects dating as far back as 2000 B.C., and the ruins of ancient Egypt, Greece, and Persia have yielded discs made of gold, glass, bone, and pottery with shank-like protrusions on the back. Although constructed like buttons, these pieces were probably used as ornaments and seals rather than fasteners.

Throughout the European Dark and Middle ages, buttons were used again primarily as decorations, or at most to fasten a loose-fitting gown or cloak at the neck with the aid of a loop or toggle. As unbelievable as it seems, button holes were not used in Europe until some 3,500 years after the first buttons. Many costume historians credit the returning Crusaders with bringing the concept of the button hole back from the Middle East, where it had been in use among the Saracen cultures for some time.

Throughout the Renaissance, the button became a herald, a barometer of sorts of the wearer's social status. Kings, queens, and other nobility were prolific in their use of luxurious buttons. In 1520, King Francis I of France ordered 13,400 buttons from his jeweler. They were sewn onto a black velveteen suit, which he wore to a meeting with Henry VIII of England, hoping to impress him into an alliance. When Henry VIII himself went to meet Anne of Cleves, his third wife, he wore great buttons of diamonds, rubies, and Oriental pearls. But it was France's King Louis XIV, the infamous Sun King, who perhaps reached the zenith of button excess: He spent $6 million on buttons during his reign and $600,000 in one year alone!

The 18th century ushered in the "Golden Age" of the decorative button, a time when not only noblemen but the more prosperous members of the rising middle classes could advertise their status with large and finely

This Page and Opposite Page: All of the button cards in our museum feature actual and often rare period buttons. The single button card, for instance, holds an authentic George Washington inaugural button, while the bird card holds a complete aviary of stamped brass and porcelain bird Victorian buttons, circa 1880-1900.

The French Revolution

"I Protect the Nation"

"Long Live the Nation"

"Liberty or Death"

"The French Republic 1797"

"Live Free or Die"

crafted buttons of enamel, carved ivory, jasperware, reverse-painted glass, and lustrous pearl. True, the glitter may have come from strauss (rhinestones) or faceted steel rather than diamonds, but the appearance was grand never the less. It seems odd to us now, however, that only 18th-century men sported these highly decorated buttons on their frock coats; women at the time still fastened their gowns with lacing or hooks and eyes.

Indeed, buttons did not become important to women's dress until the mid-19th century. By mid-century, advances in technology made an amazing number of materials commonly available for button making: horn could be heated in molds; rubber could be vulcanized or hardened; shell buttons could be intricately carved with steam-driven presses; and flat sheets of brass could be stamped into detailed pictures or designs. Celluloid, the first synthetic plastic, arrived in the 1870s and was used to imitate ivory, horn, tortoise shell, marble, and even jade. Tintypes were made into buttons for tiny, portable keepsakes.

During this time, men's clothing was becoming more standardized as women's fashions exploded into a riot of ornamental excess and ostentatious display. Women's clothing buttons fully participated in this trend and the multiplicity of designs is mind-boggling by today's standards. Picture buttons, mass-produced in stamped or molded brass and white metal, lifted motifs from every possible source: novels, operettas, history, mythology, the zodiac, monuments such as the Eiffel Tower, and every type of flower, plant, and animal known to man. Even flies, spiders, and alligators made their way onto buttons.

A fashion also grew around reproducing some of the most popular buttons of the 18th century 100 years after their first use. In particular, French factories recreated the lovely champlevé enamels of the 1700s, though the floral and pastoral designs were

This Page and Opposite Page: All of the button cards in our museum are decorated with Victorian paper scraps donated by our late friend and antiques collector, Stephanie Smythe. The button cards feature themes and materials of buttons, from insects and fruit to glass, metal, and plastic.

now more often created with decals rather than hand painting. Cut steel, the brilliantly faceted buttons first made by Matthew Boulton in the 1700s to imitate diamonds and marcasites, returned to vogue.

But perhaps the button most emblematic of this era is the Victorian "jet." Almost always made of black glass rather than the mineral jet, these buttons were popularized by Queen Victoria during her extended (42-year) period of mourning, which began in 1861 after Albert, the Prince Consort, died. These pressed glass buttons—which, when held to the light appear to be dark amethyst glass rather than black—were created in hundreds, if not thousands, of patterns in small household workshops in Bohemia.

By comparison to the 18th and 19th centuries, the story of buttons in the 20th century lacks in romance and variety. By the 1920s, the simple four-hole button made of pearl, bone, glass, or plastic had become the standard in both men's and women's clothing. The zipper, invented in 1893, became increasingly popular and functioned as perhaps an apt symbol of the streamlined and sped up lives we began to lead in the 20th century. The simple, four-hole button has perhaps now become a nostalgic symbol for simpler, slower times. The wringer washer, modern dry-cleaning methods, and, later, the automatic washer and dryer were all the enemies of ornate buttons.

Only during the 1930s and '40s was there a brief flowering of novel and eccentric buttons. New synthetic materials made possible the

production of flamboyantly carved and molded designs. Bakelite, invented in 1907 by Leo Baekeland, came in a range of stylish colors and could be sliced, laminated, and carved to create the bold and striking Art Deco buttons that are so coveted by collectors today.

Catalin plastic, introduced in the 1930s, rapidly overtook Bakelite because of its ability to be molded rather than just carved. Catalin and Bakelite were both used to create what have long been my very favorite sort of buttons: the whimsical buttons known to collectors as "realistics" or "goofies" because they are made in the realistic shape of the item they represent and they often exude an exuberant, humorous style that is indeed "goofy."

Perhaps it was the rigor of living through the Depression and World War II years that made women want to decorate their dresses with buttons representing all varieties of fruits and vegetables, clothespins, fish, pencils, rulers, blackboards, cigarette packages, horse heads, roosters, and lobsters, to name only a very few designs. These novelty buttons are avidly sought by collectors today and often command higher prices than the older Victorian buttons.

The 1950s and early 1960s—decades that saw the near-universal spread of the automatic washer and dryer—yielded only one kind of interesting button: the gorgeous, sparkling luster glass button created in Germany.

At the end of World War II, Bohemian glass workers fled from Czechoslovakia across the newly formed Iron Curtain into Bavaria, where they set up their glass bead and button-making workshops and began exporting well-made glass buttons to the rest of Europe and the United States. These heirs of the Victorian Bohemian glass makers used historic techniques to create glittering gold and silver luster glass buttons, and silky, shimmering "moonglows," which combined clear and opaque glass in cloud-like swirls. Out of vogue during the 1970s through the 1990s, these buttons are again being made in Germany. They are joined by a great wave of glass buttons coming from the born-again glass factories of the Czech Republic, which have seen new life with the fall of the Iron Curtain.

Prosaic and utilitarian, today's buttons give little hint of the glories of their ancestors. The historic buttons available to us now in quantities great enough to find affordably and transform into jewelry—those made between 1850 and 1950—are the subject of the remainder of this book. Perhaps it is because I was a journalism/English major rather than an art student that I am drawn to these buttons just as much for their stories as their beauty. As you look through these projects, try to imagine the lives these buttons led the last 50 to 120 years, the gowns they graced, and the family tragedies and triumphs they witnessed. Then imagine the new lives they will lead, adorning heirloom jewelry you have made for your own pleasure or to give as a treasured gift.

Bettie Gandy Garrett, my father's ?, who at age 95 gave me much of the inspiration for this business. Born in 1889, a child of Reconstruction and a woman of the Depression, she saved everything, including about 20 boxes of buttons. It was while rummaging through these boxes with her that the idea for Grandmother's Buttons was born.

Chapter 1
Getting Started

While it is much easier to turn buttons into jewelry when you snip off the shanks, doing so removes any value the button may have as a button. And those values have been growing at astounding rates! By any conservative estimate, the buttons I buy today to transform into jewelry cost some 2,000 times more than they did in 1985. Their worth is now such that it makes no sense to sabotage their "button value" by taking the shanks off. Therefore, we will show you many tricky ways to accommodate or hide the shanks while making jewelry. Of course, two- or four-hole sew-through buttons, bless them, have no such problem.

Many would claim that the most important technique we could teach is *how* to find such lovely old buttons. For 20 years, I have heard a constant chorus of: "Where in the world do you come across all of these buttons?" My answer is always that they are still out there; they're just getting more difficult to find. The first, most obvious, and easiest method is the Internet and the various on-line auction services. There are also state and national button-collecting societies that would be very happy to introduce you to their hobby; just be sure to reassure them that you will leave all buttons intact.

The other usual haunts of the button collector—antique shows and shops, flea markets, garage sales, fabric stores with vintage stock—are yielding fewer treasures, though they are always worth pursuing. Don't forget to explore the most personally meaningful resource—your family's button boxes. I am often saddened at shows when customers lament, "We just threw out our grandmother's button tins when we cleaned out her house. Nobody wanted them then."

In creating projects for this book, we tried to use representative examples of buttons from the general period between 1850 and 1950 that can be commonly found today, albeit with some serious button sleuthing and at times not insignificant expenditures on your part. Know that you can also design fabulous jewelry using less aged but still attractive buttons from the 1960s through today—buttons that can be found at every flea market and garage sale in the world. What is important is that the buttons you use speak to you, that they connect you to some interior sense of nostalgia, whimsy, or aesthetic yearning. It may be a color, material, texture, or shape that pulls you in, but be assured that you will find enough buttons with charm and history to assemble something marvelous. And remember, if all else fails, you can always buy button jewelry from us on our website, www.grandmothersbuttons.com.

Particular Betty's Button Box

My Buttons always are in place
For I am a lady of good taste

Sears, Roebuck and Co.
SOLE DISTRIBUTORS

Supplies

Following is a list of items used throughout this book. You will want to make sure to have all of the necessary "ingredients" on hand before beginning any of the projects.

BEADS

There has never, ever been a better time to buy beads for crafting than today. The Internet has allowed anyone with spare change and overseas contacts to become a bead importer, and some beautiful, eccentric, and affordable beads can be found on-line.

We list a number of the larger and more stable catalog and on-line bead suppliers at the back of this book, but feel free to put any kind of bead we recommend—say, perhaps 20 mm turquoise donut—into an Internet search engine to see what you find.

Photo A: Austrian crystals—These are authentic 32 percent lead oxide crystal beads faceted by hand to create a mirror-like sparkling finish. They are expensive, but dazzling.

Photo B: Czech glass beads—In the Introduction we explored the rebirth of the Czech bead and button industry after the fall of the Iron Curtain. I find it fascinating that the great-great grandchildren of the Bohemians who created Victorian glass buttons and beads are making them again today and shipping them by the container load to the United States and China. Often these Czechs use materials and techniques that have changed little in two centuries. Fire-polished beads are created by pressing glass in a mold to make the beads, which are roughly faceted by hand or machine. A better luster is then created by re-heating the beads, which slightly melts or rounds off the facets. Fire-polished beads emulate the sparkle of crystal at a more affordable price, and also come in many striking iridescent finishes.

Photo C: Natural stone beads—The veritable avalanche of imported beads from China, India, Thailand, and other developing countries has made beads created from natural or semi-precious stones much more affordable than they were in the past. Keep in mind that many of the more affordable strands are actually dyed versions of less valuable stones. For example, jasper is often dyed to look like turquoise and called "African turquoise" while serpentine is dyed and called "new jade." All reputable bead dealers will tell you the difference. We are very fond of African turquoise and new jade and have used both in many projects throughout this book. It's perfectly acceptable to use dyed or heat-altered beads as long as you like them and know that is what you are using.

FINDINGS

Photo D: The term used for jewelry hardware, findings, includes the pieces and parts that aren't beads used to create jewelry. Pictured are many of the types of findings used in the projects throughout this book. Be aware that when a finding is silver in color it can usually be purchased in either sterling silver or base metal, depending on the quality you want and the amount you are prepared to spend.

Base metal is the generic name for non-precious metals such as brass, pewter, white metal, and steel used in jewelry. Base metal findings are often plated in gold or silver and can be quite handsome.

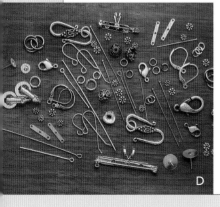

MATERIALS

Photo E: Bead caps—Stamped or cast metal "caps" that can be threaded on top of a bead for extra ornamentation.

Photo F: Bead wire—Multi-strands of ultra-thin wire twisted together and encased in a plastic coating to create a strong but flexible strand for bead stringing. When buying, remember that the more strands of wire encased, the more flexible the bead wire is. We use .12" and .18" diameter, 7-strand bead wires in these projects, which is the least number of strands you will want to use.

Photo G: Chain—We prefer antique brass to shiny gold-plate chain (it complements the aged brass patina of the buttons), and are equally fond of antiqued sterling and silver-plate. If you cannot find a chain to your liking, be sure to pick over the junk jewelry stalls at flea markets, or even go through your old jewelry box. Re-purposed chain is perfect for button jewelry projects.

Photos H and I: Collaging bases—Round, perforated bases onto which one wires beads and buttons to create a collage. They come with pronged backs that attach to cover the tangle of wires or to glue on pin or earring backs.

Photo J: Crimp bead—A small, soft metal bead in silver or gold that is squeezed, or crimped, around a loop of bead wire to hold it to a clasp.

Photo K: Disc/loop bracelets—The original button jewelry bracelet, this is an inexpensive bracelet that has been used by most button jewelry makers for decades. It has flat discs or sometimes squares onto which you may glue the button, which are connected by jump rings. Best used with flat, sew-through buttons.

Photo L: Earring clips—Glue-on backs needed to support heavy earrings or for clip-on earrings.

E

I

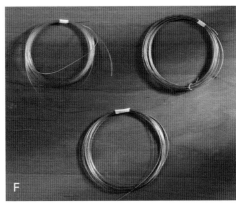

F

J

G

K

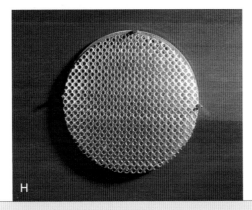

H

L

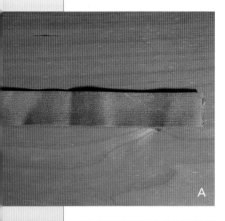

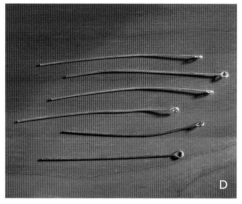

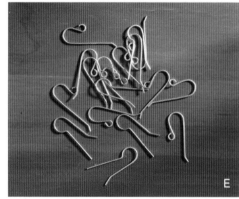

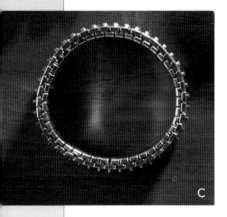

Photo C: Expandable link bracelet—Sometimes called a "cha-cha" bracelet, these expandable link bracelets have one, two, or three rows of loops for attaching beads, buttons, or charms. Normally they are 7" in diameter, stretching to 9".

Extender chain—Light chain in 2" lengths added to a necklace so that a lobster claw can attach to it to make the necklace longer.

Photo D: Eye pin—A long, straight piece of wire that has a loop at one end. Used to thread bead(s) onto; the other end is then clipped and formed into another loop. Often used to link beads together in a chain. Thicker eye pins, 28 gauge or so, can simply be turned. Thinner eye pins, 21 gauge or less, will need to be wrapped to be secure. Eye pins are available in 1"-3" lengths. We have not specified lengths in these projects because you can easily trim a longer pin to work for almost any purpose.

Photo E: French ear wire—An elegant earring wire also called a "fish hook." Commonly available in plated base metals, sterling, gold-filled, and gold. French wires without loops are for adding a bead and making a loop under the bead.

Photo F: Earring posts—A flat, metal disk with an earring post attached that can be glued onto the back of a flat button to make an earring. You also need a back to thread over the post to hold it onto the ear.

Photo G: Head pin—A long, straight piece of wire with one end finished with a flat or ball end—much like a straight pin without a point. Beads can be strung on them, and the other end cut and formed into a loop to create a bead dangle. (When using thinner head pins, 21 gauge or less, you will need to wire wrap these loops for security.) As with eye pins, we have not specified lengths in these projects because you can easily trim a long head pin to serve your purpose.

Photo A: Elastic cording and banding—Stretchy cotton-covered elastic cord or woven banding found in the sewing or notions sections of stores.

Photo B: Eurowires—A very handy kind of earring wire with a folding lever in the back that keeps the earring from falling off of the ear. Available in base metal, sterling, and gold-filled from most jewelry supply catalogs.

Photo H: Hook and eye closures—A graceful necklace closure with hand-crafted appeal.

Photo I: Jump ring—Small round or oval wire ring that can be opened and closed to link pieces of the jewelry together. The jump rings in these projects range from 4½-9 mm in diameter.

Photo J: Lobster claw—Our favorite sort of open-and-close clasp; named for obvious visual similarities.

Pin back—A bar, catch, joint, and pin stem put together in one unit that can be glued onto the back of a piece to make a brooch.

Photo K: Pin back with bail—A special pin back that has a necklace bail attached to the top so the piece can be worn as a pendant or brooch.

Photo L: Ring and toggle—A bracelet and necklace closure made with a ring on one end and toggle sized to fit through the ring on the other. Many people worry that pieces made with ring and toggle closures are likely to fall off; we have not found that to be the case.

Photo M: Stampings—Thin pieces of metal (usually brass) that have been stamped and cut in a die to create a decorative piece of metal. We just love stampings at Grandmother's Buttons, particularly since we have discovered that the original dies for many of the stampings still available today were cut almost a century ago.

Photo N: Strand spacer: A thin bar with a number of holes in it used to keep in place multiple strands in a necklace or bracelet.

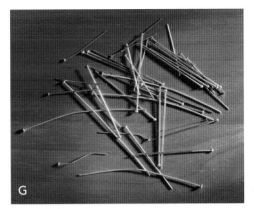

G

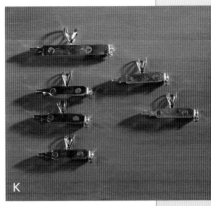

K

H

L

I

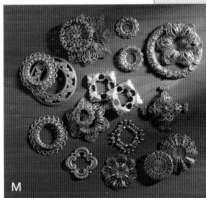

M

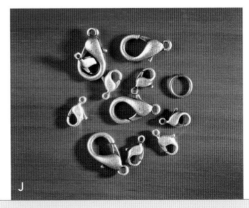

J

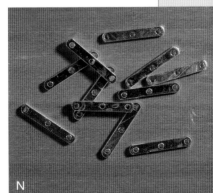

N

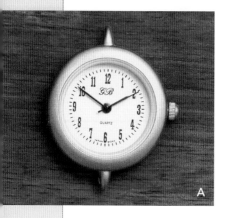

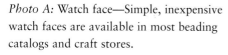

Photo A: Watch face—Simple, inexpensive watch faces are available in most beading catalogs and craft stores.

SHANK "DISGUISERS"

Photo B: As I mentioned, we are always on the hunt for round, donut-shaped items to nestle a button into and thereby accommodate or hide its shank. Natural stone donuts, cloisonné donut beads, O-shaped mother-of-pearl pendants, circular metal stampings or filigrees, and even Chinese coins all fall into this category. Beads can also be strung in a circle into which a button can be placed. Don't hesitate to use your imagination to come up with even more useful "shank-hiding" objects and techniques.

TOOLS

You will need only the most basic of bead-stringing and jewelry-making tools to create the projects in this book. Below is the whole list:

Photo C: Chain-nose pliers—All-purpose pliers that can be used to open and close jump rings and other findings.

Photo D: Concave/round-nose forming pliers—These pliers are the easiest way to make small loops at the ends of head pins and eye pins.

Photo E: Round-nose pliers can also be used for this purpose.

Photo F: Crimping pliers—Pliers with two indentations in the jaw that allow you to form strong and neat crimps to secure the ends of strung bracelets and necklaces.

Photo G: Jewelry glue—This is our preferred type of adhesive for joining buttons to stampings or other buttons because this type of glue never dries rock-hard. While it creates a strong bond, it retains a flexibility that allows you to later pull the button from the other piece with no harm to the button (that is, if sparing amounts are used).

Photo H: Scissors—Used for cutting bead wire and thread.

Photo I: Wire cutter—Used to cut heavier wire, head pins, and eye pins.

Strong-hold glue—Thin, rapid drying glue used to secure knots in stretch jewelry cord.

Toothpicks—For applying jewelry glue.

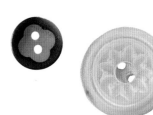

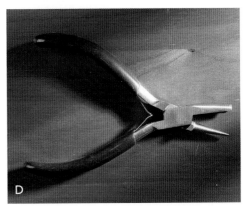

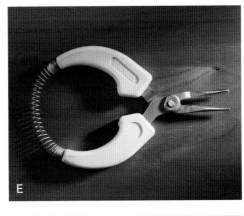

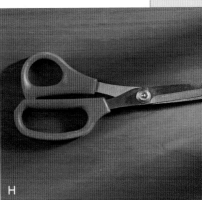

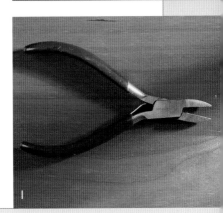

Techniques

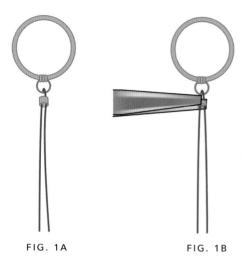

FIG. 1A   FIG. 1B

FIG. 2A

FIG. 2B

FIG. 2C

CRIMPING

Thread one crimp bead on one end of length of flexible beading wire. Thread one end of clasp. Bring wire back through crimp, leaving 3" tail. Slide crimp base close to clasp, leaving small space. Mash crimp hard in hole closest to handle, which looks like a half moon.

Hold wires apart so one piece is on each side of deep dent. (See Fig. 1A.) Put dented crimp in front hole of pliers, standing it on end, and mash as hard as you can. This folds crimp into a small cylinder. (See Fig. 1B.)

MAKING LOOPS OR EYES

Cut wire, leaving ⅜" tail above bead. Bend wire against bead at right angle with tip of chain-nose pliers. (See Fig. 2A.)

Grip top of wire in round-nose pliers. If loose, loop will be teardrop shape. (See Fig. 2B.)

Without pulling, rotate wire into loop as far as your wrist will turn. Release, then re-grasp loop at same place on pliers. Keep turning wire to close loop. The closer to the tip of the pliers you work, the smaller the loop will be. (See Fig. 2C.)

ALTERNATE METHOD USING CONCAVE/ROUND-NOSE FORMING PLIERS

Slide beads onto head pin or eye pin. Position forming pliers where wire comes out of bead. Squeeze wire to form loop with pliers.

Using your fingers or chain-nose pliers, bring wire around to form complete loop. Trim excess wire with cutter pliers and finish loop.

WIRE WRAPPING BEAD TO MAKE DANGLE OR CHAIN LINK

You will want to use this process when using wire that is 21 gauge or thinner for security.

Thread bead onto middle of length of wire. Bend each end at 90-degree angle to bead. (See Fig. 3A.)

Using round-nose or forming pliers, bend each end into loops. (See Fig. 3B.) Grasp loop firmly with one pair of chain-link pliers and use another pair to wrap end of loop tightly around wire. (See Fig. 3C.) Do this once with head pin to make dangle, or twice with length of wire to make chain link.

WIRE WRAPPING TWO- OR FOUR-HOLE BUTTON TO MAKE DANGLE OR CHAIN LINK

Insert eye pin into top hole of button; bend so eye is positioned slightly above rim of button. (See Fig. 4A.)

Holding eye with one pair of chain-nose pliers, take end of wire in another pair of pliers and wrap around other wire, just below eye. (See Fig. 4B.)

After wrapping two to three loops, trim wire flush with wrapping. This creates a charm or dangle. (See Fig. 4C.)

To create button link for chain, repeat this procedure through bottom hole of button.

MAKING BEAD DANGLE

Slide bead(s) onto head pin (for dangle) or eye pin (for bead chain link). Using chain-nose pliers, bend wire to form right angle as close to bead as possible. Trim excess wire using wire-cutter pliers, leaving about ⅓" of wire.

Grab very end of wire with round-nose pliers and roll wire around tip of pliers to form a circle centered over wire stem.

To open or close this loop, move wire gently out to side using chain-nose pliers. This makes a small opening to link piece to ear wire, another chain link, a jump ring, etc. Do not pull loop straight out, as this will distort the round shape of loop.

FINISHING BRACELETS OR NECKLACES

All of the strung bead pieces in this book (with the exception of the more complex peyote stitch seed bead projects) are done on bead wire. Here is our preferred way of finishing a bead wire piece:

- Cut piece of bead wire about 6" longer than finished length of your project. String beads onto wire. Note: We often put tape at one end of the wire as we string beads. That way we can add or subtract beads from both ends of the project until we are completely satisfied with it.

- Thread crimp bead onto bead wire on one end of piece, followed by ring, toggle, jump ring, or lobster claw clasp.

- Bring bead wire back through crimp bead and through first few beads of bead strand.

- Pull wire until beads and clasp are snug.

- Use crimp pliers to secure crimp bead; squeeze bead first in back indentation of pliers, and then crimp it again in first indentation.

- Trim end of wire so it is hidden in beads.

SURGEON'S KNOT:

This is a secure knot used to finish projects strung on stretch bead cord. You may want to put a drop of strong-hold glue on the knot to add additional strength.

- Cross the right end of the elastic cord over the left and go through the loop. Go through again. Pull the ends to tighten. Cross the left end over the right and go through once. Pull the ends to tighten.

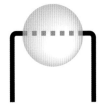

FIG. 3A

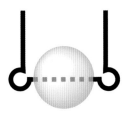

FIG. 3B

FIG. 3C

FIG. 4A

FIG. 4B

FIG. 4C

Chapter 2
Victorian Metal Buttons

What do a rooster playing the guitar and Mary Queen of Scotts have in common? Both have been the subject of Victorian metal picture buttons, along with almost every character of classical mythology, most members of the plant and animal kingdoms, and an amazing number of historical figures from the 17th through the 19th centuries. When it came to ornamenting their lavish gowns with dozens and dozens of buttons, the whimsy of Victorian women evidently knew no boundaries.

It is hard for the modern mind, so used to thinking of pantyhose as the greatest allowable encumbrance upon a woman's movement and comfort, to imagine what it took for a woman of the late 19th century to get dressed: corsets to be laced, various undergarments to be fastened with hooks and eyes and drawstrings, and last but hardly not least, two to three dozen buttons to be fastened down the front and sleeves of her gown. It is thanks to this prolific use of buttons that Grandmother's Buttons can even exist today.

The buttons used in this chapter's projects are primarily floral and "conventional"—rather than pictorial—metal buttons made between 1870 and 1910, the late Victorian and Edwardian eras. Brass was used more than any other material to make both "conventional" and pictorial buttons; large, thin sheets were stamped by steam-driven presses to create button blanks, which were then bound to a brass back pierced by a twisted wire shank. Many Victorian metal buttons are made in two, three, or even more layers, with accents of pewter, faceted steel, glass, or fabric combined with the brass.

We are often asked where Victorian metal buttons were made. In the United States, Connecticut was the button-making center with the firms of Waterbury, Scovill, Lane, and Cheshire all located there, while France, Austria, Germany, and England were the European centers of manufacture.

Please remember that the buttons we have used are antique originals. When preparing to make your projects, do not try to find exact duplicates of our buttons. Instead, find buttons that speak to you, that will complement the colors and styles of beads you have chosen. After all, your buttons and our buttons will certainly have one thing in common—they will have lived a past life on clothing and in a world that we can only imagine.

Brass & Cut-Steel Filigree Button Necklace & Earrings

The formal, ornate style of this necklace and earrings set makes it the most Victorian or Edwardian looking project in this book. One can almost imagine Queen Alexandra, King Edward's wife, wearing it to a state ball, though of course her necklace would have been of actual diamonds and gold, not the cut steel and brass that was first made to imitate the sparkle of diamonds.

Photo A: The beads and buttons shown here are used in creating the necklace.

Opposite Page: This fairly simple and straightforward necklace will take on different characteristics depending upon the intricacy and sparkle of the buttons you use.

Brass & Cut-Steel Filigree Button Necklace

BEADS & BUTTONS
- Antique brass and cut-steel filigree buttons: ⅝", 2
- Antique brass and cut-steel filigree buttons: 1", 3
- Fire-polished Czech gemstone rondelles: brown iris, 12 x 9 mm, 19
- Fire-polished Czech teardrop beads: black diamond, 13 x 10 mm, 3
- Metal bead: gold, 2 mm, 1
- Spacer beads: daisy, antique gold, 4 mm, 38

MATERIALS
- Extender chain: 2"
- Eye pins: gold, 19
- Filigree bead cap: antique gold, 3
- Head pin: gold
- Jump rings: gold, 4½ mm, 24
- Lobster claw: antique gold
- Pliers: chain nose, round nose, wire cutters

INSTRUCTIONS
Make 16 single-bead chain links. Thread one 4 mm spacer, one rondelle, and one 4 mm spacer onto eye pin. Use pliers to form loop on other end of eye pin. Make two two-bead chain links. Thread one teardrop bead, one filigree bead cap, one 4 mm spacer, one rondelle, and one 4 mm spacer onto eye pin. With pliers, form loop on other end of eye pin. Repeat once to form second link.

Form two-bead drop. Repeat above instructions one time, replacing eye pin with head pin.

Form necklace side strands. Connect bead links with filigree buttons using jump rings in this order: five rondelle links, one two-bead link, one 1" button, one rondelle link, one ⅝" button, one rondelle link. Repeat to form other side of necklace.

Connect each strand to remaining 1" button at 10 o'clock and 2 o'clock on button, using jump rings.

Connect two-bead drop to bottom 1" at 6 o'clock by opening loop on drop and closing it over edge of button.

Attach lobster claw to right side bead chain using jump ring. Attach extender chain to left side bead chain using jump ring.

Photo A: The beads and buttons shown here are used in creating the earrings.

Opposite Page: This necklace also would be stunning created with brightly colored beads. For a dramatic effect, use a larger teardrop bead.

Brass & Cut-Steel Filigree Button Earrings

BEADS & BUTTONS

- Antique brass and cut-steel filigree buttons: 1", 2
- Fire-polished Czech gemstone rondelles: brown iris, 12 x 9 mm, 2
- Fire-polished Czech teardrop beads: black diamond, 13 x 10 mm, 2
- Metal beads: gold, 2 mm, 2
- Spacer beads: daisy, antique gold, 4 mm, 4

MATERIALS

- Filigree bead cap: antique gold, 2
- French ear wires: gold, 2
- Head pin: gold, 2
- Pliers: chain nose, round nose, wire cutters

INSTRUCTIONS

Thread one 2 mm metal bead, one teardrop bead, one filigree bead cap, one 4 mm spacer, one rondelle, and one 4 mm spacer onto head pin. With pliers, form loop on other end of head pin. Repeat once to form second link.

Open loop at top of two-bead drop and place over bottom of 1" button. Close. Repeat with second drop and button.

Open loop of French ear wire and place over top of 1" button. Close. Repeat with second ear wire and button.

BUTTON BASICS
Identifying the Age of a Button

One of the quickest ways to ascertain the age of a metal button is to turn it over and examine its back. If it has a looped or twisted wire shank embedded in a metal back, it is very likely a button made prior to 1918 (the year after which button collectors classify a button as "modern" rather than "antique"). Self-shank buttons—those in which the metal back is actually shaped into a protrusion through which a hole is made—can be either antique or modern. Modern self-shank buttons, however, are generally very lightweight in construction and are usually hollow.

Bunches of Brass Buttons Bracelet & Earrings

Though it looks complex, this bracelet is actually a very simple design, requiring only chain, jump rings, two pliers, dozens of buttons, and a fair amount of patience to create it. We've chosen a variety of brass, steel, pewter, and enamel buttons along with fire-polished Czech glass beads to execute this piece, but the design can be effective with all sorts of buttons as long as they have a thin or wired shank. I have seen fabulous examples done with jet glass, carved pearls, and even plastics. The earring set also is simple to make, yet stunning in design.

Photos A and B: The beads and buttons shown here are used in creating the earrings and the bracelet.

Opposite Page: Victorian brass buttons were often tinted blue, green, or garnet; beautiful cluster bracelets can also be made with the green and garnet buttons and accented with various shades of green and garnet beads.

Bunches of Brass Buttons Bracelet

BEADS & BUTTONS
- Antique buttons (brass, cut steel, pewter, glass, and enamel): ½"-1", 36
- Fire-polished Czech glass gemstone rondelles: blue opal, 9 x 6 mm, 2
- Fire-polished Czech glass round: blue iris, 8 mm, 2
- Fire-polished Czech glass round: light sapphire, 8 mm, 2
- Fire-polished Czech glass teardrop: cobalt, 13 x 10 mm, 3
- Spacer beads: daisy, antique gold, 4 mm, 9

MATERIALS
- Bracelet chain: antique gold, about 44 links, 7⅝", 1
- Head pins: gold, 9
- Jump rings: gold, 4½ mm, 48
- Pliers: chain nose, round nose, wire cutters
- Ring and toggle set: antique gold

INSTRUCTIONS
To create bead dangles: Thread one glass bead and one spacer bead onto head pin and turn with round nose pliers to create dangle. Repeat until 9 dangles are made.

Using jump rings, attach one button to each chain link, leaving last four links on each end empty.

Go back and add bead dangle with jump ring approximately every four to five links. Finish bracelet by adding ring closure at one end and toggle at other end with two jump rings.

BUTTON BASICS
Getting the Right Look

It will take some time to attach buttons to the chain link as you will want to experiment with spacing of the buttons, i.e. alternating large, medium, and small buttons, or evenly distributing the buttons with blue accents and/or cut-steel glitz. If you have used a majority of large buttons, you will probably not be able to fit all 36 buttons on the bracelet. If you have mostly small buttons, you may need a few more buttons and may occasionally need to put two buttons per link.

Bunches of Brass Buttons Earrings

BEADS & BUTTONS

- Antique sew-through pearls: dyed blue, ¾", 2
- Fire-polished Czech glass round: blue iris, 8 mm, 2
- Fire-polished Czech glass teardrop: cobalt, 13 x 10 mm, 2
- Spacer beads: daisy, antique gold, 4 mm, 6

MATERIALS

- Eye pins: gold, 6
- French wire earrings: gold, 2
- Head pins: gold, 2
- Pliers: chain nose, round nose, wire cutters

INSTRUCTIONS

Turn sew-through buttons into links using head pins and wire wrapping technique. Turn blue iris beads and spacer beads into links using head pins. Make bead dangles with teardrop beads using head pins and spacer beads. Open loops and link all four parts of each earring together. Close loops.

Collage Brooch & Earrings

Costume jewelry artist Miriam Haskell was famous for wiring glass, pearlized, and metal beads to perforated bases in the 1940s and '50s. We've made our brooch with antique pearl and metal buttons and an old watch-case "locket" with a photo of my grandmother inside (the grandmother of 30-plus boxes of buttons). The earrings feature a pretty button instead of a watch case.

Photo A: The beads and buttons shown here are used in creating the brooch and the earrings.

Opposite Page: This black silk shirtwaist hails from the same era as the buttons we've wired to this brooch. Before donating or throwing away vintage clothes, be sure to check for interesting buttons.

Below Right: The pronged back of the brooch hides all of the beading wire underneath.

Collage Brooch

BEADS & BUTTONS

- Antique brass button: 1¾", 1
- Antique carved sew-through pearl buttons: 1", 2
- Antique metal or pearl buttons: ⅜"-½", 4
- Antique rhinestone button: 1"
- Fire-polished Czech glass beads: copper luster, 6 mm, 4
- Fire-polished Czech glass beads: rose luster, 4 mm, 12
- Freshwater pearls: khaki potato, 5 mm, 18
- Glass pearl beads: khaki, 8-10 mm, 2
- Round Czech glass beads: rose luster, 6 mm, 10
- Seed beads: brown iris, size 06, 36

MATERIALS

- Beading wire: .012", 1 yard
- Brass-domed collaging base: gold, 56 mm or 2¼"
- Glue-on pin back: 1½"
- Pronged back for collaging cage: gold
- Scissors
- Vintage photo: reduced to fit inside watch case
- Vintage watch case: gold

INSTRUCTIONS

Remove back from watch case (you may need a small screwdriver to pry it open); take watch workings out. Place photo, reduced and cut to size, behind watch crystal. Snap back onto case.

Thread one end of beading wire through two holes on collage base, from rear to top and rear again. Tie short end off onto long end and then trim short end.

Build up base of beads from 3 to 6 o'clock and 9 to 12 o'clock on collage base, working same wire through collage base holes over and over. Attach four of largest buttons with wire; attach watch "locket" to sew-through pearl buttons, threading wire through sew-through holes.

Finish design by filling in blank areas with strands of smaller beads and buttons. When satisfied with collage, tie off remaining wire in back and trim.

Place pronged back over back of collage base to hide wires and crimp prongs. Glue pin back to back side of collage. Let dry.

Collage Earrings

BEADS & BUTTONS

- Antique brass button: ½", 2
- Fire-polished Czech glass beads: copper luster, 6 mm, 6
- Fire-polished Czech glass beads: rose luster, 4 mm, 28
- Freshwater pearls: khaki potato, 5 mm, 14
- Round Czech glass beads: rose luster, 6 mm, 10
- Seed beads: brown iris, size 06, 18

MATERIALS

- Beading wire: .012", 2 feet
- Brass domed collaging base: gold, 22 mm, 2
- Pronged back with ear clips (for collaging base): gold, 2
- Scissors

INSTRUCTIONS

Tie off beading wire onto collage base. Experiment with threading or "sewing" beads onto base, taking care to have bead patterns reflect one another as you work on second earring.

Using bead wire, sew one button on each earring on base of beads you have built up. Add few more beads around button; tie bead wire off on back of base.

Position and crimp pronged backs with ear clips onto each base.

Photo A: The beads and buttons shown here are used in creating the earrings.

Above: Once the beads and buttons are wired to the base, simply position the pronged backs with ear clips to the collaging base and bend the prongs into place. All the messy wires are now hidden away.

Opposite Page: We found it close to impossible to create absolutely matching earrings using this free-form style. Their one-of-kind beauty is what makes them interesting!

BUTTON BASICS
Designing Free-Form

This is a free-form piece of jewelry, so you really must experiment, threading or "sewing" strands of 4-6 beads at a time onto the collage base. This will not be a speedy project! In the instructions, I have listed the exact number and type of beads I used, but you will need to have many different buttons and beads on hand to achieve the look you want. Trust trial and error and your own artistic eye. You may also want to experiment with this quicker way of creating a collage brooch: simply glue layers of buttons, vintage glass cabochons, and even rhinestones onto the brass frame. You won't be able to use beads with this method, but the cabochons and rhinestones will add their own sparkle.

BUTTON BASICS
Adapting a Pin Design

Few jewelry-making distributors carry these old-style pierced collaging backs. If you have trouble finding them, however, you can substitute a slightly domed filigree stamping. When you have finished wiring your beads and buttons onto the stamping, simply glue a flat piece of metal or plastic to the back, onto which you can then glue a pin back.

Glass Pearl Bead & Button Medallion Necklace & Earrings

Photo A

If you have difficulty stringing on the buttons along with the beads in this project, you may also string the necklace using just the beads, and glue the buttons onto the tops of the pearl bead medallions. This is not as secure as stringing the buttons on, but it is much, much easier. As the earrings are small, the buttons are glued to the surface of the beads.

Glass Pearl Bead & Button Medallion Necklace

BEADS & BUTTONS
- Antique brass buttons: ½", 7
- Crimp beads: gold, 2
- Lamp-work round glass beads: flecked gold, green, topaz, silver, 8 mm, 28
- Metal beads: gold, 2 mm round, 63
- Pearlized glass beads: round, 8 mm, 28
- Spacer beads: daisy, antique gold, 4 mm, 112

MATERIALS
- Bead wire: 30" strand
- Extender chain: 2" length
- Lobster claw clasp: antique gold
- Pliers: chain nose, crimping, round nose, wire cutters

INSTRUCTIONS
Attach lobster claw to strand of bead wire with crimp bead. String one 4 mm spacer, one 8 mm lamp-worked bead, one 4 mm spacer, and one 2 mm gold bead onto bead wire. Repeat four times.

String one 2 mm gold bead, one 4 mm spacer, one 8 mm pearl bead, one 4 mm spacer, one 2 mm gold bead, and one 4 mm spacer onto remaining two wires.

Separate the two wires. Leave one loose; onto other wire, string one pearl bead followed by these beads: spacer, gold bead, spacer, pearl bead, spacer, gold bead, spacer, and pearl bead.

Thread button onto loose wire. Take ends of the two wires in your hand, pull pearl beads around into circle, and insert both wires into 4 mm spacer and 2 mm gold bead. Leave enough play in wire with button so it will sit in center of rosette.

Run both wires through first spacer, pearl bead, and spacer combination to form pearl rosette.

Next, place 2 mm gold bead on wire, then 4 mm spacer, 8 mm lampwork bead, and 4 mm spacer. Repeat two times.

Create another pearl bead rosette as described in steps above, then follow it with another section of three lamp-work beads separated by 4 mm spacers and 2 mm gold beads. Repeat this step five more times.

Finish stringing necklace by adding five more lamp-work beads separated by 4 mm spacers and 2 mm gold beads.

Attach extender chain to this end of necklace using crimp bead. If buttons do not sit exactly in middle of pearl rosettes, secure them with bit of jewelry glue or epoxy.

Photo A: The beads and buttons shown here are used in creating the necklace and earrings.

Opposite Page: The classic design of this set makes for versatility in wearing. The necklace and earrings would look equally beautiful dressed up with a little black dress or casual with jeans and a button-down shirt.

Glass Pearl Bead & Button Rosette Earrings

BEADS & BUTTONS

- Antique brass buttons: ½", 2
- Metal round beads: gold, 2 mm, 8
- Pearlized round glass beads: 8 mm, 8
- Spacer beads: daisy, antique gold, 4 mm, 16

MATERIALS

- Brass wire: thin, 3" lengths (not bead stringing), 2
- Earring posts: glue-on with 14 mm pads, 2
- Jewelry glue
- Scissors

INSTRUCTIONS

Thread onto thin brass wire: one pearl bead, one 4 mm spacer, one 2 mm gold bead. Repeat four times.

Bring wire back through first pearl bead; pull so rosette is snug. Pull that wire under rosette and twist with other loose end of wire. Trim.

Using generous amounts of jewelry glue, adhere button to top of rosette. Let dry, making sure that none of glue shows from top of earring.

Turn earring over and adhere post to back, once again using generous amounts of glue. Repeat entire process for second earring.

BUTTON BASICS
Pearls of Wisdom

Instead of using glass pearl beads for these projects, use real or faux pearls. Many of us have strands of pearls that go unworn because they are too short or too long or perhaps the strand is broken. Make sure to adjust the size of the other beads to complement your pearls if necessary.

Cut-Steel Button Charm Watch

• •

I've often felt part magpie, so drawn am I to bright, shiny objects. Perhaps that is why cut-steel buttons please me so much, and why I am so fond of the bracelet watch created by Joanna McLemore. Joanna started with a handful of small faceted steel buttons, circa 1900, then added chain and fire-polished hematite glass beads to produce a show-stopper of a watch.

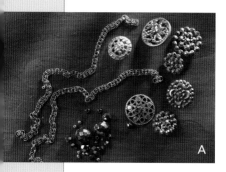

Photo A: The beads and buttons shown here are used in creating the watch.

Opposite Page: Both formal and festive, this watch is not nearly as difficult to make as it appears.

Cut-Steel Button Charm Watch

BEADS & BUTTONS

• Antique cut-steel buttons: ½"-¾", 5
• Fire-polished Czech glass round: hematite, 4 mm, 13
• Fire-polished Czech glass round: hematite, 6 mm, 14
• Fire-polished Czech glass round: hematite, 10 mm, 5

MATERIALS

• Chain: 5" strand, antique silver, 4 mm thick, 2
• Head pins: silver, 32
• Jump rings: silver, 4½ mm, 21
• Pliers: chain nose, crimping, round nose, wire cutters
• Watch face: silver with rings for connecting on each side

INSTRUCTIONS

Create basic form of watch by linking ring and toggle, watch, and chains using these steps:

Attach toggle to 12 o'clock end of watch using two jump rings. Attach three jump rings to 6 o'clock end of watch. Leave third jump ring open and place one end of each chain on that jump ring. Close jump ring.

Bring other two ends of chain together with jump ring. Use another jump ring to attach ring part of clasp to last jump ring.

Turn all fire-polished beads into bead drops by stringing them on head pins; turn and trim head pins to form loops.

Attach all fourteen 6 mm hematite beads to 5" chain by opening loop on each bead head pin, putting it over link in bracelet, and then closing loop. Space these beads evenly on chain.

Attach five antique buttons to second 5" length of chain, using two jump rings each and spacing evenly.

Attach all five 10 mm hematite bead dangles to 5" chain, alternating with buttons and using jump rings.

Attach three 4 mm hematite bead dangles to jump rings at ring end of watch. Attach two 4 mm hematite bead dangles to jump rings at toggle end of watch.

Attach seven 4 mm hematite bead dangles to jump rings at 6 o'clock end of watch.

Midsummer Midnight Necklace

. . . .

Made by Anna Macedo, this sculptural neckpiece features a large scarab button. The button is an inspiration in itself for its size—it's just under 2" in diameter—and the realistically designed raised-relief scarab with embedded marcasites. Anna thought to surround the scarab with deep colors to enhance the glow of its burnished metal finish. She created drama in the use of glittering crystals and tinted pearls, and added textural interest in juxtaposing matte beads with metals and reflective glass beads. The whole effect is that of a moonlit and mysterious treasure.

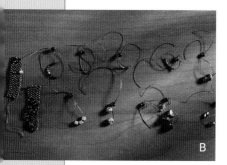

A

B

C

Photos A, B, and C: The beads and buttons shown here are used in creating the necklace.

Opposite Page: The star of this sculptural necklace is the incredible scarab beetle button. It is worth investing in a unique button when gathering materials for this project.

Right: While working on your jewelry piece, occasionally take the project to a mirror with excellent lighting. Study the piece, make notes of the flaws, and adjust beading as needed.

BEADS & BUTTONS
- Beads: bronzed gold, #13, 1 small bag
- Bugle beads: iris, purple, multicolored, 1 tube
- Charlottes: #13 metallic dark bronze, 1 hank
- Crystal beads: smoky bronze, 5 mm, 5
- Crystal faceted beads: clear, 4 mm, 1 strand
- Crystal faceted beads: pale green, 2 mm, 2 strands
- Delica beads: 1 small bag each
  -#312 dark brown/multi (matte, opaque)
  -#022 deep gold
  -#002 midnight blue/multi
  -#465 dark blue/green/multi
- Faceted oval beads: bronze metallic, 4 mm, 1 strand
- Glass cubes: matte green and copper, 5 mm, tube of each
- Iridescent opaque glass leaves: olive green, 10
- Opaque glass leaf: bronze metallic, large

- Scarab button: large
- Seed pearls:
  -dark blue/green, 1 hank
  -bronze, 5 mm, 1 hank
- Specialty brass knots, filigreed barrels, and other interesting beads, 12-15
- Teardrops: dark bronze, 4 mm, 1 strand
- Translucent glass beads: cobalt blue, 4 mm, 1 strand
- Triangle tubes: metallic bronze, 3 mm, 1 tube
- Victorian brass buttons with marcasites, 2-3
- Victorian button (for clasp)

MATERIALS
- #12 beading needles, 2-3
- Beading thread: style B, black, 1 spool
- Cuticle scissors
- Jewelry glue
- Scissors (suitable for cutting suede)
- Suede: black, 3" square

INSTRUCTIONS

Apply thin coat of jewelry glue to both button back and suede. Let jewelry glue cure for a minute, then gently press button onto suede. Leave to dry overnight.

When adhesive is completely dry, peel excess jewelry glue from edges of suede and trim suede to edges of button. (See Fig. 1.) Leave tiny fraction (about 1/16"-1/8") around button to allow surface for inserting needle.

Note: Blanket stitch (See Fig. 2, a-e.) will be used to make row of #11 brown beads around circumference of centerpiece button.

The blanket stitch: Insert needle into suede at button's edge, going from back to front of button. The first stitch will be to anchor the thread. Put needle through loop of thread from front to back, and pull up tight. Go back into suede from back to front. String one bead and insert needle into suede again, from back to front, just one bead's width away. Again, put needle through loop from front, and tighten. Be sure bead sits up with its hole parallel to edge. Continue this method until you have beaded circumference of button, all along suede edge. Keep stitches uniform to assure neat appearance. Thread needle through all beads on edging and pull up slack to make them line up perfectly.

Add subsequent rows of beads using peyote stitch. (See Fig. 3.) Remember to increase by a bead or two each row as you build out from centerpiece. After few rows of #11 brown beads, you will be ready to begin to add other, more decorative beads to your stitch. Use your own creativity and good judgment, and have a ball.

Note the centerpiece in progress. You can see the rows of #11 brown beads, and where we've added large and small crystals, a ladder of bugle beads, some square beads, and other decorative elements into the peyote stitch. Remember that you can change the color of the basic #11 beads within your peyote stitch to add interest and flash. In this piece we've added rows of gold beads and sprinkled dark blues and greens into our rows. You can also come back and add pearls, large beads, buttons, sparklies, and other elements on top of the rows of #11 beads, too.

When your basic centerpiece is completed to your satisfaction, decide where you want to attach your necklace portions. Thread needle with 20"-30" of thread, and anchor securely in a likely place at edge of centerpiece of beads; then create your necklace as you wish. Use four or six beads in peyote stitch to make thin strap, or string strands of beads, or do a combination of both. At ends of necklace portions, create clasp by securing button at one end, and loop of small #13 beads at other.

Examine your necklace for errant thread ends. Snip loose threads or fibers closely with cuticle scissors. Gently polish with a clean, slightly damp cloth to remove any mild residue.

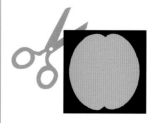

FIG. 1

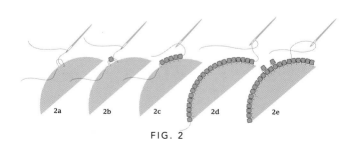

2a   2b   2c   2d   2e

FIG. 2

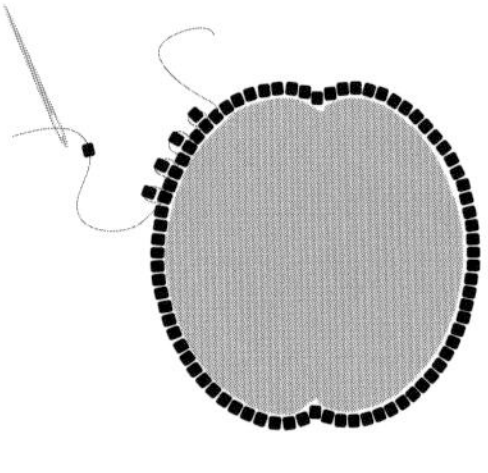

FIG. 3

Natural Stone Donut Charm Bracelet & Earrings

When we began planning for this book, we ordered several bags of natural stone donuts in assorted sizes and materials. They proved to be invaluable, both for their ability to impart color to a project and to provide a convenient hiding place for the button shanks. The 20 mm donuts in this project, unlike the larger ones, are also used as beads, drilled with holes and sold strung on 16" strands.

Photo A: The beads and buttons shown here are used in creating the bracelet.

Opposite Page: Shown here like a miniature necklace, this charm bracelet is made with an assortment of our favorite Czech beads. We encourage you to shop for your own favorite assortment of rich colors and interesting shapes and textures.

Natural Stone Donut Charm Bracelet

BEADS & BUTTONS
- African turquoise donut bead: 20 mm
- Antique brass buttons: ½", 3
- Antique brass buttons: ¾", 3
- Ball beads: gold, 2 mm, 15
- Carnelian faceted beads: 10 mm, 2
- Cushion-cut turquoise/green Czech glass beads: 14 mm, 2
- Fire-polished amber Czech glass rondelles: 9 x 7 mm, 2
- Lamp-work glass beads: gold, green, brown, 10 mm, 2
- Oval faceted Czech glass beads in topaz with turquoise or green: 16 mm, 3 (can substitute 16 x 12 mm fire-polished teardrop beads)
- Poppy jasper donut beads: 20 mm, 2
- Rhyolite donut bead: 20 mm
- Spacer beads: daisy, antique gold, 4 mm, 33

MATERIALS
- Charm bracelet chain: antique gold, with about 21 links
- Filigree stampings: round, antique gold, with centers cut out, 3
- Head pins: gold, 16
- Jump rings: gold, 4½ mm, 22
- Pliers: chain nose, round nose, wire cutters
- Ring and toggle set: antique gold

INSTRUCTIONS

Create four charms with natural stone donut beads in this manner: On head pin, thread 2 mm gold ball bead, two 4 mm daisy spacer beads, and bottom hole in donut bead.

Slip shank of ½" antique button over end of head pin while it is in "donut hole." Thread end of head pin through hole in top of donut bead, then thread one 4 mm spacer bead and one 2 mm ball bead on top of donut. Turn head pin with pliers to create loop. Do this three more times.

Create three charms with filigree pieces in this way: Using cutting pliers cut center from round filigree pieces, taking out about ⅜"-½". Glue ¾" button on top of each filigree piece. Do this two more times.

Create charm with each bead in this way: Onto head pin, thread 2 mm ball bead, 4 mm spacer bead, glass or stone bead, another 4 mm spacer bead, and another 2 mm ball bead. Turn head pin with pliers to create loop. Do this total of 12 times until all beads are used.

Attach each charm to link of charm bracelet with jump ring in this order: rhyolite donut charm, oval faceted Czech glass bead, lamp-work glass bead, filigree charm, turquoise cushion-cut bead, carnelian faceted bead, poppy jasper donut charm, oval faceted Czech glass bead, fire-polished amber Czech glass rondelle, filigree charm, turquoise cushion-cut bead, lamp-work glass bead, turquoise donut charm, faceted carnelian

bead, oval faceted Czech glass bead, filigree charm, fire-polished amber Czech glass bead, turquoise cushion-cut bead, poppy jasper donut charm.

Attach ring and toggle closure to ends of bracelet with jump rings.

Poppy Jasper Donut Button Earrings

BEADS & BUTTONS
- Antique metal button: ⅜"-½", 2
- Cushion-cut turquoise/green Czech glass beads: 14 mm, 2
- Poppy jasper donut beads: 20 mm, 2

MATERIALS
- Earring posts (on 10 mm pads), 2
- Head pins: gold, 4
- Jewelry glue
- Pliers: chain nose, round nose, wire cutters

INSTRUCTIONS
Insert head pin into lower hole of poppy jasper donut, entering from inside of donut. With pliers and cutter, make and trim loop where head pin leaves donut.

To make bead dangle with the turquoise bead, thread it on head pin and make loop at top of bead. Join loop on bead to loop on donut and close loops. Glue buttons to center of donuts. Let dry.

Turn over and glue earring post over donut hole. Let dry. Do each step again for second earring.

Photo A: The beads and buttons shown here are used in creating the earrings.

Right: The antique metal buttons were chosen for this project because they complement the colors of the stone donut beads.

Opposite Page: Imagine how different this style of earring would look with onyx donuts, silver buttons, and ruby red beads. The color and material combinations that would look striking are almost endless.

Natural Stone Strung Bracelet, Earrings & Pendant

A sister piece to the Natural Stone Donut Charm Bracelet, this piece is somewhat smoother and easier to wear. Don't stress out if you have difficulty finding 20 mm donuts in these exact materials—African turquoise, poppy jasper, and rhyolite—simply choose among the colors you can find to create a pleasing combination. We have made the earrings in two types of donuts—rhyolite and turquoise—to show you the flexibility of these designs.

Photo A: The beads and buttons shown here are used in creating the bracelet.

Opposite Page: Select a group of ½-inch Victorian brass buttons that complement one another to create this natural stone donut strung bracelet, pendant, and earrings set.

Natural Stone Strung Bracelet

BEADS & BUTTONS

- African turquoise donut beads: 20 mm, 2
- Antique brass buttons with wire shanks: ½", 6
- Crimp beads: gold, 2
- Fire-polished amber Czech glass rondelles: 9 x 7 mm, 7
- Poppy jasper donut beads: 20 mm, 2
- Rhyolite donut beads: 20 mm, 2
- Spacer beads: daisy, antique gold, 4 mm, 14

MATERIALS

- Bead wire: .018" diameter, 10" length
- Jewelry glue
- Jump rings: gold, 4½ mm, 2
- Pliers: crimping
- Ring and toggle set: antique gold
- Toothpick

INSTRUCTIONS

Thread 4 mm daisy, amber rondelle, and 4 mm daisy onto bead wire. Insert bead wire through first hole of poppy jasper donut. Insert bead wire (which is in donut hole) through button shank, then insert it into second hole of jasper donut.

Repeat this process five more times, using stone donuts in this order, after poppy jasper: rhyolite, African turquoise, poppy jasper, rhyolite, African turquoise. Finish strand with 4 mm daisy, amber rondelle, and 4 mm daisy.

Attach ring to one end of bracelet using crimp bead. Attach toggle hooked onto two jump rings to other end of bracelet (jump rings allow toggle to pass through ring).

Secure buttons to top of each donut with bit of jewelry glue applied with toothpick. Let dry.

BUTTON BASICS
How Natural are Natural Stone Beads?

Natural stone donut beads are widely available and easy to find. Some are truly in their natural state—human hands have touched them only for carving, shaping and polishing. Others have been further manipulated by man in terms of dying or heat treating. Reputable dealers will be forthcoming in how their products are made. Of the donuts used in this project, the rhyolite and poppy jasper are natural, whereas the African turquoise is dyed. In fact, it is not turquoise at all, but rather serpentine dyed a greenish-turquoise shade. African turquoise, while not truly natural, is attractive and affordable.

Rhyolite or Turquoise Donut Earrings

BEADS & BUTTONS

- Antique buttons with wire shanks: ½", 2
- Fire-polished amber Czech glass rondelles: 9 x 7 mm, 2
- Red jasper beads: 4 mm, 2
- Rhyolite (or turquoise) donut beads: 20 mm, 2
- Spacer beads: daisy antique gold, 4 mm, 4

MATERIALS

- French ear wires (without loops): gold, 2
- Jewelry glue
- Pliers: chain nose, round nose, wire cutters
- Toothpick

INSTRUCTIONS

Thread bottom hole of donut bead onto head pin. While top of head pin is in donut hole, string button shank onto it; thread it through top hole of donut bead.

Thread 4 mm spacer, amber rondelle, and another 4 mm spacer on top of donut bead. Turn top of head pin with pliers to create loop.

Thread 4 mm red jasper onto long stem of unturned ear wire. Trim wire to ¼" below bead and turn with pliers to form loop.

Open loop of bead/button drop and join to loop of ear wire. Close loop.

Secure button to donut bead with bit of jewelry glue applied with toothpick. Let dry. Repeat process for second earring.

Poppy Jasper Donut Pendant

Instead of drilling a hole in the donut, we attached a backing to create the pendant. You can use a pretty ribbon or gold chain to hang pendant for necklace.

BEADS & BUTTONS

- Antique brass or brass and cut-steel button: 1" or 1½"
- Poppy jasper donut: 40 mm

MATERIALS

- Filigree stamping: gold, 1¼"
- Jewelry glue
- Jump ring: gold, 4.5 mm
- Necklace: gold, 18"
- Necklace bail: gold
- Pliers: round nose

INSTRUCTIONS

Using jewelry glue, attach button to top of poppy jasper donut, centering so button shank fits neatly into donut hole. Let dry.

Glue donut to gold filigree stamping, taking care to center donut. Let dry. Attach necklace bail to filigree with jump ring. Slip necklace chain through bail.

Photos A and B: The beads and buttons shown here are used in creating the pendant and earrings.

Opposite Page: The reds, greens, blues, and tans of the poppy jasper, rhyolite, and African turquoise stone beads used in these pieces complement the aged colors of these 19th-century volumes, which are actually the same age as the brass buttons used.

Oriental Button & Carnelian Bracelet, Necklace & Earrings

Clay and jewelry artist Nancy Rothschild has had a long and serious love affair with Oriental design and culture, as evidenced by her several trips to China (from one of which she returned with her lovely daughter, Mei). When Nancy agreed to create a project for this book, we of course culled our box of Oriental-themed buttons to give her for inspiration. The brass buttons she used were made between 1880 and 1910, and reflect that era's fascination with all things Oriental, inspired primarily by the success of Gilbert and Sullivan's "The Mikado" in 1885 and Puccini's "Madame Butterfly" in 1905.

Photo A: The beads and buttons shown here are used in creating the bracelet.

Opposite Page: A form of banded agate, carnelian beads come in colors ranging from bright rust to translucent cream to reddish brown. These pieces look best when made with such variegated carnelian beads, as Nancy has done here.

Oriental Button & Carnelian Bracelet

BEADS & BUTTONS

- Antique brass buttons with Oriental themes: ½"-¾", 9
- Carnelian beads: faceted round, 6 mm, 8
- Carnelian beads: off-round, 10-12 mm, 12
- Carnelian beads: smooth round, 4 mm, 37
- Carnelian beads: smooth round, 6 mm, 6
- Carnelian beads: smooth round, 8 mm, 8
- Crimp beads: gold, 2
- Seed beads: brown iris, size 06, 20
- Seed beads: jet black, size 08, 24

MATERIALS

- Bead wire: 1' strands, .012" diameter, 3
- Pliers: crimping
- Ring and toggle set: gold
- Scissors
- Spacer bars with three holes: gold, 1" long, 3

INSTRUCTIONS

To begin bracelet, place all three bead wire strands together with ends flush. String crimp bead onto all three strands, followed by toggle closure. Bring strands back through crimp bead, then pull about ½" beyond crimp bead so that crimp bead is snug against toggle. Crimp with pliers.

Thread one 6 mm smooth round carnelian bead over all six strands. Trim remainder of short end of strands even with bead. String one button onto all three strands.

Separate three strands and string them, left to right, in this order: (left and right strands) three 08 jet black seed beads, one 6 mm faceted round carnelian, one off-round 10-12 mm carnelian; (middle strand) three 08 jet black seed beads, one 4 mm carnelian, one 6 mm smooth round carnelian, two 06 iris seed beads. Place spacer bead over all three strands.

For next section, string three strands this way: (left and right strands) one 10-12 mm off-round carnelian, one 4 mm carnelian, one 8 mm carnelian, two 4 mm carnelians, one 06 brown iris seed bead, antique button, one 06 brown iris seed bead, two 4 mm carnelians, one 8 mm carnelian, one 4 mm carnelian, one 10-12 mm off-round carnelian; (middle strand) one antique button, two 06 brown iris seed beads, one 4 mm carnelian, one 6 mm faceted round carnelian, one 4 mm carnelian, one 8 mm carnelian, one 4 mm carnelian, one 6 mm faceted round carnelian, one 4 mm carnelian, one 6 mm smooth round carnelian, two 4 mm carnelians, two 06 brown iris seed beads, and one antique button followed by a spacer bar. Repeat these instructions in mirror fashion to complete bracelet.

Finish bracelet by stringing crimp bead onto all three strands of bead wire, pulling strands through ring of ring clasp, inserting them back into crimp bead, and pulling until bracelet is snug. Crimp and trim.

Photo A: The beads and buttons shown here are used in creating the earrings.

Opposite Page: Among the Asian-inspired operas, operettas, and folk tales represented in these buttons are: Gilbert and Sullivan's The Mikado (1885); Madame Chrysantheme by Messager (1893); and the Blue Willow story of Chinese folklore (featured on countless china plates and platters).

Oriental Button & Carnelian Necklace

BEADS & BUTTONS
- Antique brass Oriental-themed buttons: ½"-¾", 16
- Antique brass Oriental-themed button: ⅞"
- Carnelian beads: round, 4 mm, 2
- Carnelian beads: round, 6 mm, 2
- Carnelian beads: round, 8 mm, 18
- Crimp beads: gold, 2
- Seed beads: brown iris, size 06, about 80

MATERIALS
- Bead wire: .018" diameter, 20"
- Pliers: crimping
- Ring and toggle set: gold
- Scissors

INSTRUCTIONS
Put tape on one end of 20" strand of bead wire. String one 4 mm carnelian, one 6 mm carnelian, and two brown iris seed beads onto wire.

String one of smaller antique buttons, two more brown iris seed beads, one 8 mm carnelian, two more brown iris seed beads, and another button onto wire.

Continue stringing beads and buttons so four to six seed beads are under each button (they do not show from front) and each button is separated by one 8 mm carnelian.

Work necklace so one ⅞" button is in middle of strand, forming focal point of necklace. Use two carnelian beads to frame this focal button.

When you have strung last button, finish necklace with two brown iris seed beads, one 6 mm carnelian, and one 4 mm carnelian. Attach ring to one end and toggle to other using crimp bead.

Oriental Button & Carnelian Earrings

BEADS & BUTTONS
- Antique brass Oriental-themed buttons: ¾", 2
- Carnelian round beads: 4 mm, 12
- Carnelian round faceted beads: 10 mm, 2
- Spacer beads: daisy, antique gold, 4 mm, 2

MATERIALS
- Eye pins: gold, 2
- French ear wires: gold, 2
- Head pins: gold, 2
- Pliers: chain nose, round nose, wire cutters
- Strong-hold glue

INSTRUCTIONS
String three 4 mm carnelian beads onto eye pin. String one button onto same eye pin, followed by three more 4 mm carnelian beads.

Form loop at top of eye pin using pliers. Open loop on French wire and attach to top of bead and button eye pin. Close loop.

On head pin, string one 4 mm spacer, one 8 mm carnelian bead, and one 4 mm spacer. Use pliers to form loop at top of head pin. Attach this loop to loop at bottom of bead and button eye pin. Repeat to form second earring.

Put several drops of strong-hold glue on back of earring where eye pin goes through button shanks and beads. This will keep button from spinning about on the earring.

Pearls, Buttons & Cuff Links Charm Necklace & Earrings

Photo A: The beads and buttons shown here are used in creating the necklace.

Opposite Page: Other treasures from the jewelry and sewing boxes that can be used in such assemblage necklaces are: old bracelet charms, religious medals, small thimbles, and broken dangle earrings.

I once saw a section in a button collector's web site dedicated to the odd items that she and fellow collectors had found while digging through button tins. Along with baby teeth, religious medals, and loose beads, it seems they often found single cuff links. Since a lone cuff link has little value without its mate, we feel no remorse in instructing you to clip the backs off the three (single) antique cuff links you will need to create this necklace.

Pearls, Buttons & Cuff Links Charm Necklace

BEADS & BUTTONS

- Antique cuff link: smaller oval
- Antique cuff links with stones, 2
- Antique etched pearl buttons: ½"-¾", 2
- Antique filigree buttons: ⅞"-1", 2
- Antique filigree buttons: ½"-¾", 2
- Crimp beads: gold, 2
- Freshwater pearls: champagne potato, 7-8 mm, 16" strand
- Spacer beads: daisy, gold, 4 mm, 53

MATERIALS

- Antique watch fob
- Bead wire: 24" length
- Extender chain: gold, 2" length
- Eye pins: gold, 2
- Jewelry glue
- Jump rings: 4½ mm, gold, 2
- Jump rings: 9 mm, gold, 11
- Lobster claw clasp: gold
- Pliers: chain nose, crimping
- Scissors
- Stampings: small brass with ring, 3
- Vintage photograph to copy and reduce
- Vintage watch case

INSTRUCTIONS

String spacers and pearls, alternately, onto bead wire until necklace is desired length (ours is 16" and extends to 18" with chain).

Attach lobster claw at one end and extender chain at other end using crimp beads.

To prepare charms: Remove works from watch (back should pop off easily; you might need to use finger nail file or other lever to gently pry it off).

Trim old photo or one you have reduced on color copier (or on your computer) to fit into watch case. Put into case and snap back on. Thread eye pins into top holes in pearl buttons and wrap to make charms.

Snip off backs of lone-ranger cuff links using wire cutters and file flat with coarse file or dremel tool. Glue stampings to backs of cuff links with jewelry glue to make charms. Let dry.

To assemble necklace: String watch "locket" charm in center of necklace. Going out from center in each direction, hang charms in following order, using large jump rings and leaving two pearls between each charm:

- Larger filigree buttons (⅞"-1")
- Etched pearl buttons
- Oval cuff link (left side) and ¾" filigree button (right side)
- Large cuff links with stones
- ½" filigree button (left side) and watch fob (right side)

Photo A: The beads and buttons shown here are used in creating the earrings.

Opposite Page: I love the peachy-champagne color of these pearls; their warmth does so much to bring out the rosy-gold tones in the old brass buttons and cuff links. If you prefer a longer necklace, simply use a longer extension chain.

Pearl Button Earrings

BEADS & BUTTONS

- Antique etched pearl sew-through buttons, 2 (don't have to match perfectly)
- Antique filigree or openwork buttons, 2 (don't have to match, just complement)
- Freshwater pearls: champagne potato, 7-8 mm, 2
- Spacer beads: daisy, gold, 4 mm, 4

MATERIALS

- Eye pins: gold, 2
- French ear wires: gold, 2
- Head pins: gold, 2
- Jump rings: gold, 4½ mm, 2
- Pliers: chain nose, round nose, wire cutters

INSTRUCTIONS

Thread eye pins through top holes of sew-through pearl buttons and wrap to make into dangle.

Thread spacer bead, pearl, and spacer bead onto head pin and wrap to make dangle. Hang button and pearl drop from bottom of each filigree button, using 4½ mm jump rings.

Attach French wires to top of filigree buttons. Repeat for second earring.

BUTTON BASICS
Turning Watches into Lockets

The advent of the quartz watch has turned the repair and use of broken vintage wristwatches into a problematic exercise. Finding a qualified repair person is difficult at best, and who has time to rewind a watch these days, anyway? With the watch works removed (it's easy to pop the back off and pull them out), these old watches make delightful lockets, which could be hung by themselves on a simple chain or cord, or integrated into a more complex piece such as a necklace.

BUTTON BASICS
Charming Details

The types of charms that can be used for this necklace are limited only by your imagination. Other items you can look for at antiques stores, flea markets, or your own family's jewelry boxes include lockets; small keys or locks; charms from old charm bracelets; metal tags; watch fobs; even small antique game pieces. Typewriter keys could be set on round charms and hung to spell out initials.

Treasure Necklace

· ·

A nine-strand necklace richly laden with vintage buttons, beads, and charms, this piece by Anna Macedo is inspired by a fascinating but weighty necklace she saw some years ago in Santa Fe, New Mexico. In this lighter version, small Victorian red stamped metal buttons are integrated with accent beads, tiny bells, leaves, butterflies, and silver charms. The Treasure Necklace can be worn with the strands loose or twisted, for a more dense appearance.

Photo A: The beads and buttons shown here are used in creating the necklace.

Opposite Page: This nine-strand Treasure Necklace is made with Victorian metal buttons, beads, and a variety of charms. When choosing materials for your necklace, be sure to use colors that complement one another.

BEADS & BUTTONS

- Black cut-glass faceted round beads: 3 mm, 1 small bag
- Black cut-glass faceted barrel beads: 5 mm, 1 small bag
- Black matte glass beads: #11, 1 tube
- Black matte glass leaf beads, 20-30
- Black shiny charlottes: #13, 1 hank
- Bugle beads ½"-¾" long, 20-30
- Clear transparent silver-lined delicas, 1 small bag
- Copper-toned matte glass beads: #11, 1 tube
- Dark bronze metallic glass cylinders: 3 mm, 1 small bag
- Dark bronze metallic glass rondelles: 5 mm, 1 small bag
- Deep bronze shiny glass beads: #11, 1 tube
- Gold-dusted ruby red glass seed beads: #11, 1 tube
- Metallic copper charlottes: #13, 1 hank
- Metallic copper glass beads: 4 mm, 1 small bag
- Metallic copper glass oval beads: 8 x 6 mm, 1 small bag
- Metallic dark bronze glass charlottes: #13, 1 hank
- Various charms: hearts, butterflies, knots, barrels, bells, oddities, etc., various sizes, 20-30
- Victorian red cast metal buttons 9 mm, 20-30

MATERIALS

- Beading needle: #12
- Black beading thread: style B, 1 spool
- Clear nail polish
- Copper wire "S" clasp and receiver
- Cuticle scissors
- Flotsam and jetsam: silver, bronze, or copper finish
- Masking tape

INSTRUCTIONS

Clasps: Weave together 10 bugle beads, creating ladder. (See Fig. 1, page 68.) Add one row of 10 #11 deep bronze shiny glass beads across one end of ladder. (See Fig. 2, page 68.)

Row 2: Using brick stitch, add one row of 10 beads on top of Row 1.

Row 3: Skip one bead, add eight beads in brick stitch. (See Fig. 3, page 69.)

Row 4: Skip one bead and add six beads in brick stitch.

Row 5: Skip one bead and add four beads in brick stitch.

Row 6: Skip one bead and add two beads in brick stitch. (See Fig. 4, page 69.)

Attach one half of copper "S" clasp by sewing securely to top two beads. Repeat all steps, making another 10 bugle ladder and brick stitch pyramid of beads with other half of clasp attached to top two beads.

Start Stringing: Measure 40" thread. You'll want to leave plenty of extra thread at each end to work with when you thread ends into bugle beads and back through strands for strength. (See Fig. 5, page 69.)

Note: There will be 10 strands altogether. Each strand will be threaded into one of the 10 bugle beads in your clasps. Anna designed each strand with some repeating patterns.

Above: Alternate simple strands of beads in necklace to give symmetry to the piece. Space buttons so they are not clumped together when necklace is finished.

The first strand contained mainly black faceted and matte black beads, accented with motifs of ruby and copper. For example: Begin with two black charlottes, one 5 mm black faceted, one black charlotte, one 3 mm black faceted, one black charlotte, one 3 mm black faceted, one black charlotte, one 3 mm black faceted, one black charlotte, three #11 matte black beads, one black charlotte, one #11 copper, one black charlotte, 16 #11 black matte beads, one black charlotte, one #11 copper, one black charlotte—well, you get the idea. Allow variety, but remember to repeat themes or groupings of beads to add rhythm to your design.

Lay out your strands as you finish each one so you can compare length of each strand and see how strands will relate to one another. Using masking tape, secure ends to your work table. You'll want to space out buttons and larger elements so they are not all clumped when strands are hung together. Strands of our finished necklace measure 18", not counting bugles and clasps.

Alternate strands that contain many elements and strands with few or no elements so there is some visual relief in piece. (Anna even included one strand of only black #13 charlottes, and one strand of only transparent silver-lined delicas to add more sparkle and contrast.)

Attach Strands: Beginning with your chosen strand #1, thread one end through bottom of bugle bead #1. Weave thread up and through #11 beads to secure, and then thread back through strand halfway, for strength. Make knot in likely place where it can be hidden inside large bead. Dab knot with drop of clear nail polish to keep it secure.

Weave other end of strand #1 into first bugle bead in other ladder. Repeat with securing and threading back through strand approximately halfway; make knot in likely spot. Dab knot with drop of nail polish.

Repeat these steps for each remaining strand. Use masking tape to secure necklace to your work surface to keep strands from tangling and to allow you to make measurements as you work. All strands should be as close to same length as possible. You will have to add or subtract a few beads here and there to make strands equal.

Finish: Examine your necklace for errant thread ends. Snip any loose threads or fibers closely with cuticle scissors. Gently polish with clean, slightly damp cloth to remove any mild residue.

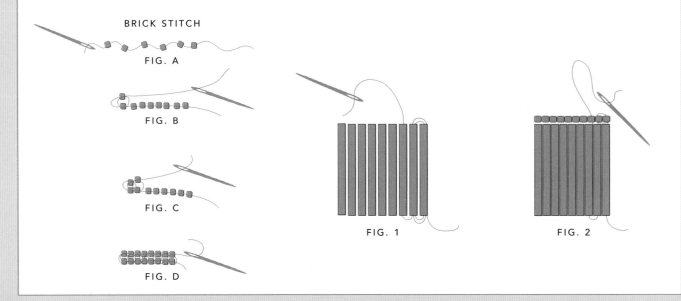

BRICK STITCH

FIG. A

FIG. B

FIG. C

FIG. D

FIG. 1

FIG. 2

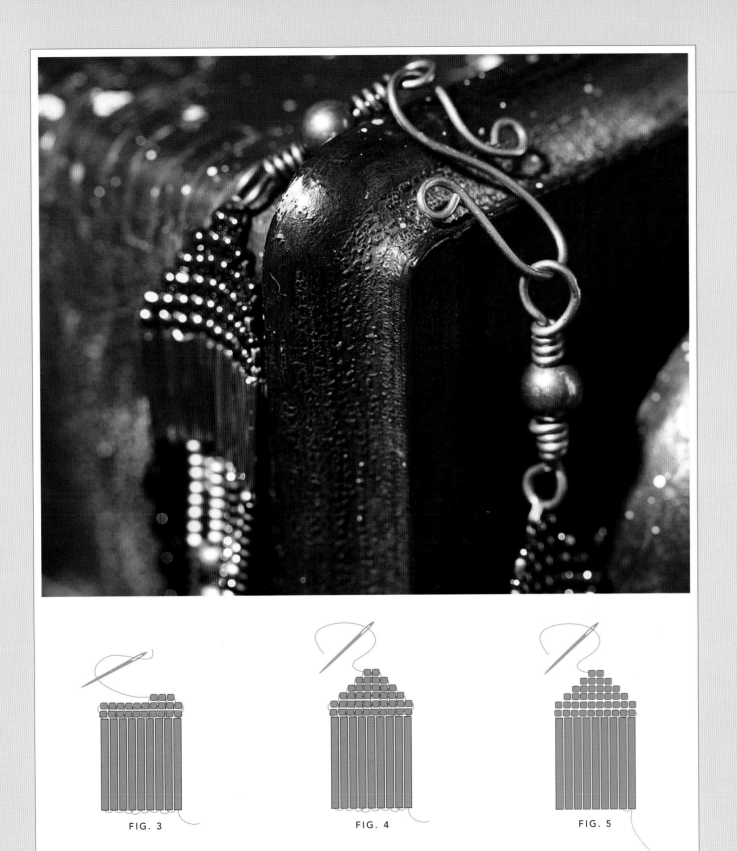

FIG. 3

FIG. 4

FIG. 5

Chapter 3
Victorian Jet Glass Buttons

Few buttons are as emblematic of the Victorian era as jet glass. When Prince Albert died in 1861, Queen Victoria went into mourning for the rest of the century and for the rest of her life. Consequently, black, or jet, was popular in all forms—especially buttons—throughout her era. The buttons and jewelry the Queen wore were made of actual jet, which is a lightweight and fragile mineral mined on England's northeast coast. True jet is very expensive, and the great bulk of the black buttons made during this time were of jet-colored glass.

Glass button making was an extensively practiced cottage industry throughout Bohemia (today's Czech Republic) during the late 19th century. Buttons were pressed by hand in iron molds, which had been cut in intricate, lacy patterns by skilled mold makers. The edges of the buttons were then ground smooth, the buttons polished, and, sometimes, gold or silver luster paint was added and fired on. All in all, 14 hand-done steps were required to create the jet glass buttons seen in this chapter.

Jet glass buttons are sometimes called mourning buttons, though true mourning buttons were those created with a matte or dull finish. A widow dared not appear with shiny or sparkling jet buttons until well into her widowhood.

So many millions of these jet glass buttons were made in Bohemia, Germany, and Austria during the late 19th and early 20th centuries that we often find patterns that we have never seen before, even after 20-plus years of button buying. Why so many buttons? Partly because it was not uncommon for a Victorian lady to ornament her gown with 40 to 60 jet glass buttons, using them not only as fasteners but as decoration and trim as well.

As with popular jewelry designs today, a successful button pattern produced by one factory was quickly copied by other factories, even factories in other countries. Occasionally one finds a black glass button with the date Dec. 28, 1880 molded onto the back. This signifies that the button was made in America using an improved button making process patented upon that date. Though American-made glass buttons were never as plentiful as European ones, they did exist and were created mainly in New York and New Jersey.

Reversible Victorian Jet Glass Button Necklace, Bracelet, & Earrings

Twenty years old, this necklace is actually one of the first pieces of button jewelry I ever made and contains a few jet glass buttons from my own grandmother's button box. At the time, I thought I was being so clever to string all of the solid jet buttons on one side and the gold luster buttons on the other so that the necklace would be reversible. I did not know that women had done this with buttons (usually sew throughs) for decades to make necklaces.

Photo A: The beads and buttons shown here are used in creating the necklace.

Opposite Page: The reversible design of this set is not a new idea by any means. Women throughout history have made two-sided necklaces as a way to accent their wardrobe without breaking their budgets.

Reversible Victorian Jet Glass Button Necklace

BEADS & BUTTONS
- Antique jet glass self-shank buttons: ⅜"-¾", 18
- Antique jet glass self-shank buttons with gold luster: ⅜"-¾", 9
- Crimp beads: gold, 2
- Fire-polished Czech glass jet beads: 4 mm, 2
- Fire-polished Czech glass jet beads: 8 mm, 22
- Fire-polished Czech glass jet beads: 10 mm, 12

MATERIALS
- Bead wire: .018", 30" length
- Extender chain: gold, 2"
- Jump rings: gold, 4½ mm, 2
- Lobster claw clasp: gold, 2
- Pliers: chain nose, round nose, wire cutters
- Scissors

INSTRUCTIONS
String eleven 8 mm fire-polished jet beads onto bead wire, followed by six 10 mm beads and one 4 mm bead.

Line up all gold luster and solid jet buttons. Arrange each in graduated strand (smallest buttons at each end and largest buttons in middle). You will follow this pattern in stringing them.

String first (smallest) gold luster button onto bead wire, followed by first solid jet button, second gold luster button, second solid jet button, and so on, alternating gold and solid jet until all buttons are strung.

String one 4 mm bead, six 10 mm beads, and eleven 8 mm beads onto wire.

Hold unfinished ends of necklace securely (so that beads and buttons do not slip off) and hold necklace up to see that it hangs gracefully. Gold luster buttons should all fall to one side of necklace, and solid jet ones to other side. Finish necklace with crimp beads, lobster claw, and extender chain.

WORDS AND MUSIC BY
GENE EMERSON

Crocheted Jet Glass Bracelet

This crocheted button bracelet pattern goes back to the Depression era, when tough times encouraged women to deck themselves out in jewelry created with nothing more than elastic thread, a crochet hook, and a box of grandmother's jet buttons. Our resident crochet artist, Susan Lindsay, made this example with some of our favorite gold luster jet buttons, but I have found samples made with both old and new metal buttons and modern glass buttons.

Above: Though jet buttons with gold luster are being made again today in Germany and the Czech Republic, it is easy to tell the authentic Victorian ones from modern styles. The antique ones are smaller and fatter, and have a gold luster that appears more like rose gold than today's brassier golds.

Opposite Page: This necklace will lie flatter on the neck and chest if one uses buttons with a similar style of rounded, self-shank back. Wire-shanked buttons will not work at all on this design.

BEADS & BUTTONS
- Antique jet glass buttons with shanks: ⅜" to ⅝", 32
- Fire-polished Czech glass beads: jet black, 32

MATERIALS
- Bead thread: black elastic, 5 yd. lengths, 3
- Crochet needle, #5
- Scissors

INSTRUCTIONS
Note: Because thread needs to be knotted together as bracelet progresses, add buttons as needed, not all at once at the start of the work. If you find that your needle eye is not small enough to pass through button and bead holes, you will need to string by hand. Finger nail polish can be used to stiffen thread tip.

Begin with thread still on the spool and measure off two yards; tie a knot. At that point begin bracelet by chain stitching 51 stitches, then joining. When piece is joined, it must be straight and lay flat.

Row 1 & 2: Chain up one and single crochet in each chain stitch, then join.

Row 3: (work in back loop of each stitch keeping the work from rolling) chain up one and slip stitch in first stitch, slide on a button and fasten into next loop. Slip stitch in next two stitches and add a button. Repeat around bracelet until 16 buttons, with two slip stitches in between, have been added. Join to complete row.

Row 4: chain one and single crochet through both loops of each stitch for 51 stitches, then join.

Row 5: repeat as in row four.

Row 6: chain one, single crochet in top of loop, add a button, single crochet in next two stitches, add another button and continue until 16 buttons have been added as in row three. Join to complete row.

Row 7: repeat as in row four.

Row 8: repeat as in row four.

Row 9: repeat as in row six.

Row 10: slip stitch all around in top loop.

Row 11: repeat as in row three using beads instead of buttons; cut thread 6" long.

On tied off portion left at beginning, string remaining 16 beads. Add as in row three. Weave ends of thread underneath and tie securely.

Jet Luster Glass Button Earrings

BEADS & BUTTONS

- Antique jet glass self-shank buttons with gold luster: ¾", 2
- Fire-polished Czech jet glass rondelles: 12 x 9 mm, 2
- Round metal beads: gold, 2 mm, 4
- Spacer beads: daisy, gold, 4 mm, 4

MATERIALS

- Epoxy glue
- Eye pins: gold, 2
- French ear wires (with loop unbent): gold, 2
- Metal dangle: gold, ½" long, 2
- Pliers: chain nose, round nose, wire cutters

INSTRUCTIONS

Thread button onto unbent wire of French wire earring. With pliers, create loop on part of wire below button shank.

Mix small amount of epoxy glue and dab on top part of wire above button shank. Arrange so ear wire lays perpendicular to button while glue dries. Repeat for other earring and let both dry.

To make bead links with fire-polished rondelles: Thread onto each eye pin, one 2 mm bead, one 4 mm spacer, one fire-polished rondelle, one 4 mm spacer, and one 2 mm bead. Create loop at end of eye pin with pliers. Do this twice.

Join top loop of bead spacers to loop under buttons. Join bottom loop of bead spacers to loop on metal dangles.

Chapter 4
Antique Mother-of-Pearl Buttons

The iconic image of a button is truly the small, simple, four-hole pearl shirt button. Today such buttons are almost invariably plastic, but the button that holds our imagination is that of our grandparents or great-grandparents—real mother-of-pearl, tiny but with a hint of luster from the nacreous lining of an ocean shell. Such buttons were made by the millions in the late 19th and early 20th centuries; to see one now is to bring back a flood of memories of those earlier times. Perhaps that is why pieces of jewelry made with these small, simple pearls always have a special appeal.

The most beautiful mother-of-pearl buttons were made with ocean shells rather than freshwater mussels. The pearl oyster shell—genus Meleagrina or Pinctada—found in the warm waters off Japan, the Philippines, South East Asia, Australia, the Red Sea, the Persian Gulf, Baja Peninsula, Polynesia, and Tahiti, produced buttons with the greatest depth of luster and the purest white color. The oyster pearl grows fairly large, 8"-10", in deep water and is always layered in colors from white to yellow to brown or gray within one shell. The white layer is considered the most desirable, although many gorgeous buttons were carved from the gray layer in the 19th century.

Abalone shells were first used to make buttons in America, and were taken from the Baja Peninsula and Japan, where they were also fished for food. Highly iridescent, abalone buttons seem to break the light into a rainbow of colors, most especially white, tan, pink, green, and purple. For that reason, abalone buttons combine beautifully with iridescent or aurora borealis beads.

This chapter has several examples of marvelously carved pearls. We are often asked if these were done by hand. The answer is both yes and no; even 100 years ago these were created with a combination of hand and machine. Steam-driven tubular saws were used to cut cylinders of shell, which were then divided into individual button blanks with a hammer and chisel. The geometric carvings were created by operators who held each individual button under a steam-driven cutting wheel. Polishing was then achieved both by tumbling in a vat and by hand. Holes were drilled with a drill press. Is it any wonder that our buttons today, even those with elaborate designs, are made of plastic?

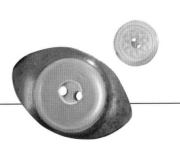

Abalone Button & Stick Pearl Bracelet, Brooch & Earrings

• •

These honey-colored buttons, shot through with the colors of the rainbow, were cut from abalone shells fished off the Baja coast of Mexico and California during the early to mid 20th century. They combine beautifully with champagne-colored stick pearls from China and iridescent fire-polished Czech rondelles.

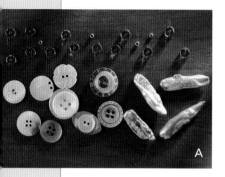

Photo A: The beads and buttons shown here are used in creating the bracelet.

Opposite Page: Our bracelet is created with an assortment of delicately etched antique abalone buttons, but a striking version can also be made with the new abalone buttons that are so plentiful today.

Abalone Button & Stick Pearl Bracelet

BEADS & BUTTONS
- Antique or vintage abalone sew-through buttons: ⅝"-¾", 11
- Crimp beads: gold, 2
- Fire-polished Czech rondelles: rose luster, 6 x 3 mm, 21
- Fire-polished round Czech glass beads: rose luster, 4 mm, 2
- Stick pearls: side-drilled, champagne color, about 1" long, 10

MATERIALS
- Bead wire, 10"
- Jump ring: 4½ mm
- Pliers: crimping
- Ring and toggle set: antique gold
- Scissors

INSTRUCTIONS

String one rondelle, one abalone button, one rondelle, and one stick pearl onto length of bead wire. Repeat this pattern until all pieces are used. Bracelet should then be about 6¾" long. (If length is too short or too long, add or subtract additional beads or buttons accordingly.)

Finish one end of bracelet by stringing one 4 mm fire-polished bead, one crimp bead, and ring part of clasp set onto wire. Bring wire back through crimp bead, crimp with pliers and trim.

Finish other end of bracelet by stringing one 4 mm fire-polished bead, one crimp bead, and toggle part of clasp set (attached to jump ring) onto wire. Bring wire back through crimp bead; crimp with pliers and trim.

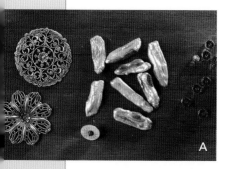

Photos A and B: The beads and buttons shown here are used in creating the brooch and the earrings.

Opposite Page: These long, free-form "stick" pearls are often mistakenly called biwa pearls. True biwa pearls come only from Lake Biwa in Japan and are fairly expensive; these somewhat similar pearls are grown in freshwater beds in China and are plentiful and affordable.

Stick Pearl Brooch

BEADS & BUTTONS

- Antique pearl and brass button: ½"-¾"
- Stick pearls: champagne color, 1¼", 7
- Stick pearls: champagne color, 1", 7

MATERIALS

- Filigree stamping: about 1⅜"
- Filigree stamping (with center removed): antique gold, about 1¼"
- Jewelry glue
- Pin back: 1½" (can use pin back with attached bail also)
- Toothpicks
- Wire clippers

INSTRUCTIONS

Arrange seven longer stick pearls into starburst pattern on larger brass stamping, leaving approximately ½" opening in center. Glue these pearls in place with generous amounts of glue using toothpick. Let dry until set.

Glue seven shorter stick pearls between each larger one to complete starburst, still leaving opening in center.

Use wire clippers to cut circle about ⅜" in center of smaller filigree. You may also need to shape filigree slightly with chain-nose pliers, pulling outer rim down to cup it a bit.

Glue smaller filigree to center of starburst. Glue antique button over hole in filigree.

(Hole allows you to leave shank on antique button. If you are using sew-through button, skip step about cutting hole in filigree.)

Let brooch dry; turn it over and glue pin back about half-way up top half of stamping.

Abalone Button & Stick Pearl Earrings

BEADS & BUTTONS

- Antique etched abalone sew-through buttons: ¾", 2
- Stick pearls: side drilled, champagne color, 1" long, 2

MATERIALS

- Eye pins: gold, 4
- French wire earrings: gold, 2
- Jump rings: gold, 4½ mm, 2
- Pliers: chain nose, round nose, wire cutters

INSTRUCTIONS

Turn stick pearls into links using eye pin and wire wrapping technique. Turn abalone buttons into drops using eye pin and wire wrapping technique.

Connect button drops with stick pearl links with jump rings.

Open loop of French wires and connect to top loop of stick pearls. Close loops.

Crocheted Carved Pearl Necklace

Photo A: The beads and buttons shown here are used in creating the necklace.

Middle: A small carved pearl button is the perfect closure for the necklace.

Bottom: This veritable bib of a necklace is made with very affordable pearl buttons.

Opposite Page: Simple crochet techniques are used so even the patient novice can create this show-stopping piece.

Friend and needle artisan Susan Lindsay crocheted this over-the-top button necklace using a whole box of cunningly carved ocean pearls from the late 19th and early 20th centuries. This is another traditional and much-loved button jewelry pattern that no one seems to know the origins of. I have seen equally stunning examples done with bone and vegetable ivory buttons, brightly colored plastics, and muted, earth-toned celluloid wafers.

BEADS & BUTTONS
- Antique shell buttons: varying sizes without shanks, 51
- Pretty button for fastener

MATERIALS
- Crochet hooks: sizes 5 and 3
- Scissors
- Silk embroidery thread, 1 spool

INSTRUCTIONS
Note: Using a larger hook for the first chain keeps the piece from curling. Switch to the smaller hook to proceed. The buttons must be laid out in a pattern before threading onto the embroidery thread. The necklace in the photograph is comprised of 15 loops. The first seven are ascending from two to five buttons and the last seven are descending from five to two buttons with the eighth loop in the center as the focal point. In working the pattern, the center button on the five and seven button loops are the same in the necklace shown.

Begin stringing the following on thread: *Row 1*, with size 5 hook, chain 140, turn. *Row 2*, with size 3 hook, one single crochet in 10" chain from hook (for button-hole) single crochet in next 40 chain. To add button, slide up button; single crochet in next chain. Chain three, add button, chain three. One single crochet in each of next five chain stitches of Row 1 (2-button loop).

Chain three, add button, chain three, add button, chain three, one single crochet in each of next five chain stitches in Row 1 (2-button loop).

Chain three, add button, repeat two more times, chain three, one single crochet in each of next five chain stitches in Row 1 (3-button loop).

Chain three, add button, repeat three more times, chain three, one single crochet in each of next five chain stitches on Row 1 (4-button loop).

Chain three, add button, repeat four more times, chain three, one single crochet in each of next five chain stitches on Row 1 (5-button loop).

Chain three, add button, repeat six more times, chain three, one single crochet in each of next five chain stitches on Row 1 (7-button loop).

Repeat five-button loop. Make another four-button loop, three button, three button, three button, two button, and two-button loop.

After last loop, make one single crochet in each of remaining chain stitches on Row 1.

Break off thread, leaving tail long enough to tie on button. Tie button on and trim thread.

Etched Victorian Pearl Link Bracelet, Earrings, & Brooch

Photos A, B, and C: The beads and buttons shown here are used in creating the bracelet, earrings, and the brooch.

Opposite Page: Who knew that natural ocean shells could produce so many hues of plum and purple? Though time enhances nature's stunning hues, new buttons also can be used.

Thin and light, etched pearl buttons such as these are often missed at the bottom of a button box. They are also sometimes so covered with the dirt of the ages that their delicate, hand-done etchings are obscured. When cleaned, they are quite beautiful. As Charles Dickens once said, "…there is surely something satisfying in seeing the smallest thing done so thoroughly."

Etched Victorian Pearl Link Bracelet

BEADS & BUTTONS
- Antique dark, etched pearl sew-through buttons: ¾", 9
- Czech glass leaf beads: iris, 12 x 9 mm, 12
- Czech glass leaf beads: opalized purple, 12 x 9 mm, 4
- Fire-polished bicone Czech glass beads: light amethyst AB, 6 mm, 5
- Fire-polished round Czech glass beads: amethyst AB, 6 mm, 5
- Fire-polished round Czech glass beads: blue iris, 6 mm, 6

MATERIALS
- Bracelet: link and loop style, with 10 oval links or pads, 1
- Head pins: gold, 32
- Pliers: chain nose, round nose, wire cutters

INSTRUCTIONS
Turn all 32 Czech glass beads into bead dangles by threading them onto head pins and turning and trimming head pins to create loops.

Glue 10 pearl buttons onto 10 pads of bracelet. Let dry. Using two chain-nose pliers, gently open link between first two pads of bracelet.

Remove one pad from link, and then string one leaf bead and one fire-polished bead on each side of ring opening. Place pad back on ring (so there are two beads on either side of replaced pad) and close ring with pliers.

Repeat this process seven times until there are four bead dangles between each of button links. As you place beads on rings, be careful to alternate colors of leaf and fire-polished beads for pleasing effect.

Above: We show the earrings with a post back here. If you prefer to have them dangle, create a loop at the top with an eye pin and attach an ear wire.

Opposite Page: The gold-plated link bracelet, brass filigree piece, and glue-on pin/pendant back can be found in many craft stores as well as large jewelry-making catalogs, both online and in print.

Etched Victorian Pearl Link Earrings

BEADS & BUTTONS
- Antique dark, etched pearl sew-through buttons: ¾", 2
- Czech glass leaf beads: iris, 12 x 9 mm, 2
- Fire-polished gemstone Czech rondelles: amethyst, 9 x 6 mm, 2
- Fire-polished round Czech glass: amethyst AB, 4 mm, 4

MATERIALS
- Earring posts: glue-on with 10 mm pad, 2
- Eye pins: gold, 2
- Head pins: gold, 2
- Jewelry glue
- Metal stamping with ring: antique gold, ½", 2
- Pliers: chain nose, round nose, wire cutters

INSTRUCTIONS
To make leaf bead dangles: Thread one 4 mm fire-polished bead, one leaf bead, and one 4 mm fire-polished bead on head pin. Repeat for second head pin. Use pliers to form loop on head pins.

Make fire-polished rondelles into links using eye pins. Glue metal stampings to back of pearl buttons so just ring shows when buttons turned over. Let dry. Glue posts onto back of buttons.

To assemble earrings: Connect bead drops to bead links by opening top loops of drops, putting them through bottom loops of dangles, then closing loops.

Open top loops of rondelle links, connect them to rings of stampings and close.

Etched Victorian Pearl Brooch with Beads

BEADS & BUTTONS
- Antique dark, carved pearl sew-through button: ¾"
- Antique dark, carved pearl sew-through button: 1¼"
- Czech glass leaf bead: opalized purple, 12 x 9 mm
- Czech glass leaf beads: iris, 12 x 9 mm, 2
- Filigree piece: round, gold, 1¾"
- Fire-polished bicone Czech glass beads: light amethyst AB, 4 mm, 2
- Fire-polished round Czech glass beads: amethyst AB, 4 mm, 7
- Fire-polished round Czech glass beads: amethyst AB, 6 mm, 2

MATERIALS
- Head pins: gold, 11
- Jewelry glue
- Pin back

INSTRUCTIONS
Thread each leaf bead onto head pin; thread one 4 mm bicone light amethyst AB bead on top of each iris-colored leaf bead.

Thread one 4 mm amethyst AB on top of opalized purple leaf bead. Make loop at top of each head pin.

Turn remaining fire-polished beads into dangles by threading each onto head pin and making loop at top of each head pin.

Open loops of all bead dangles and attach them to filigree in this order: two 4 mm amethyst AB beads, one iris leaf bead dangle, one 4 mm amethyst AB bead, one 6 mm amethyst AB bead, one opalized purple leaf bead dangle, one 6 mm amethyst AB bead, one 4 mm amethyst AB bead, one iris leaf bead dangle, two 4 mm amethyst AB beads.

Glue large button onto center of top of fililgree piece. Glue smaller button onto center of larger button. Let dry.

Turn brooch over and glue pin back in middle of top half of filigree. Let dry.

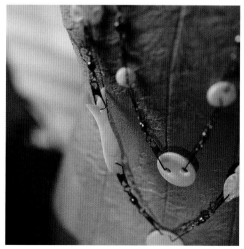

Fishing Tackle & Pearl Button Necklace & Earrings

Another interesting juxtaposition of materials, this unique necklace and earring set is adapted from a piece I bought in the late 1980s from Mississippi Gulf Coast found object jewelry artist extraordinaire Jan Hutchinson. In those years, Jan and I led a gypsy life selling our jewelry at retail holiday shopping fairs during the fall months. I was in awe both then and now of her limitless creativity.

Photo A: The beads and buttons shown here are used in creating the necklace and earrings.

Above: Though not fancy, the fishing tackle earrings possess a charm all their own.

Below Right: I love this combination of materials—buttons and fishing tackle—which at first seems an odd juxtaposition. But after all, they both relate to the sea: the buttons are made of ocean shell and the fishing tackle can be used in the surf.

Below Left: The ring and toggle clasp matches the look and feel of the tackle used to create the necklace. When creating jewelry pieces, these little details make all the difference.

Opposite Page: We were lucky enough to find one carved pearl fish ornament to make this necklace complete.

Fishing Tackle & Pearl Button Necklace

BEADS & BUTTONS
- Mother-of-pearl sew-through buttons and ornaments: ½"-1½", 10

MATERIALS
- Fishing tackle clips, 40
- Fishing tackle swivels, 20
- Jump ring: antiqued silver, ¼"
- Pliers: chain nose
- Ring and toggle clasp: antique pewter

INSTRUCTIONS
Open all clips completely. Take two opened clips per button and thread long ends of clips through sew-through holes of buttons. Use one swivel to link each clip/button/clip unit, closing clips as you go. This will create 38"-40" chain.

Connect ring to one end of chain and toggle to other. Necklace can be worn long or doubled.

Fishing Tackle & Pearl Button Earrings

BEADS & BUTTONS
- Mother-of-pearl sew-through buttons: ¾", 2

MATERIALS
- Eurowire earring wires, 2
- Fishing tackle clips, 2
- Fishing tackle swivels, 2
- Pliers: chain nose

INSTRUCTIONS
Open both clips completely. Thread one hole of each sew-through button onto long end of clip.

Thread one swivel onto top end of each clip. Close clips. Open loop of each eurowire and hang top loop of each swivel on them. Close loops.

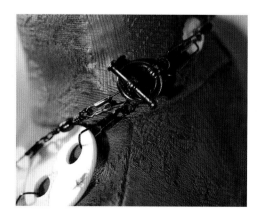

Stacked Pearl & Victorian Metal Brooches

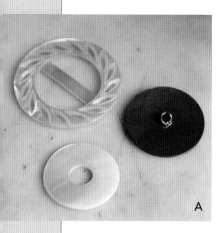

Photo A: The beads and buttons shown here are used in creating the brooch.

Right: These brooches can be made with a plain pin back, as shown here, or with a pin back with attached bail so that it can also be worn as a pendant on a chain, strand of beads or even a ribbon.

Opposite Page: The most beautiful of these brooches are those that contrast the intricate carvings of the pearl buttons with the designs of the metal ones.

The art to making these simple brooches is choosing two buttons that complement one another dramatically. Other than that, and finding a donut spacer in the right size and material, making them is quite easy.

BEADS & BUTTONS
- Antique metal button: ¾"-1¼"
- Antique pearl button: 1¼"-2"

MATERIALS
- Donut or ring spacer: slightly larger than metal button
- Jewelry glue
- Pin back

INSTRUCTIONS
Glue spacer to center of pearl button and glue metal button to center of spacer. (You may have to bend shank of metal button slightly if spacer is not tall enough to accommodate it completely.) Let dry.

Turn brooch over and glue pin back in middle of top half of back of pearl button.

BUTTON BASICS
The Allure of Enamel Buttons

Few things make a button collector's heart beat faster than a card of exceptional enamel buttons. Popular in the waning years of the 19th century, enamel buttons were considered deluxe buttons of the day and sets were often sold, like jewelry, in velvet-lined boxes.

The technique for making enamel buttons has changed little since the 16th century: Glass is reduced to a fine powder and applied to a metal surface. The glass is then melted in a kiln and fused to the metal by heat.

Most Victorian enamels were made in the champlevé style, in which the glass powder is applied to wells or hollows created in the metal by stamping it with a design. Hand-painted enamel floral and portrait designs were also very popular at this time, and are highly prized by collectors today.

It would be a tremendous mistake to clip the shank off an enamel button, but since many enamels are made in a convex shape, the shank can sometimes be gently bent under the button to make it easy to glue onto a pearl button base.

Chapter 5
Antique Porcelain & China Buttons

Few antique buttons exceed calico china, hand-painted porcelain, and stencils for charm. Their colors remind me of the soft, much-loved cottons and linen these buttons were sewn onto.

Of these three, calico buttons are the oldest, dating back to the 1840s, when an Englishman named Richard Prosser patented an inexpensive method of creating porcelain buttons from dry china-clay powder. Soon these ivory-white buttons were being decorated with transfer prints that reflected the miniature geometric dots, flowers, and checks of calico fabrics.

Calico fabrics and buttons were both very popular in the young nation of America, and the colors were those of women's clothing of the frontier: brown, lavender, black, green orange, pink, and red. Collectors are mad for calico buttons, and have identified some 326 different designs used to make them.

Because of this popularity and their age, calico buttons have risen greatly in price in the past few years, but they are worth searching out and investing in a handful because they make such charming jewelry.

In the 18th and early 19th centuries, the fine porcelain houses of Europe, particularly Meissen, Sevres, and Wedgwood, all created floral porcelain buttons of great beauty. The porcelain buttons we've used here date from a bit later, the late Victorian era through the Edwardian era, primarily 1890 to 1920. For the most part, they were home decorated by young women who hand painted porcelain button blanks; this was a popular lady's hobby craft, much like embroidery or crocheting.

We find many of these buttons with the painter's initials on the back, identification for when they were sent off to a commercial kiln to be fired. As with most hobby crafts, the skill of the artisans varied, and it is fun to search for those samples with truly beautiful roses, violets, pansies, and forget-me-nots.

Stencil buttons are the 20th-century grandchild of calicos. Made in Czecho-Slovakia, Germany, Austria, and France during the 1920s and '30s, these white and ivory two- and four-hole china buttons boast geometric, bold patterns that clearly reflect an Art Deco influence. The popular colors—blue, green, brown, lavender, black, pink, and orange—remind one of the colors found in brightly patterned quilts of the same era. Though quite collectable, stencils are definitely more affordable than calicos.

Beaded Calico Button Bracelet & Earrings

The idea to tie two flat, sew-through buttons together with stretchy bracelet cording to form a button "bead" came to me on one of the many break-of-day walks I practiced to clear my mind to work on this book. An amazingly simple but effective technique, I think you could tie all sorts and sizes of sew-through buttons together to create a range of funky "beads."

Photo A: The beads and buttons shown here are used in creating the bracelet.

Opposite Page: If calico buttons prove too hard to find, this bracelet can also be made with lovely little carved pearl buttons.

Beaded Calico Button Bracelet

BEADS & BUTTONS
- Antique calico china buttons: just under ⅜"–⅝", 17
- Assorted beads: 36 total
  - Chinese lamp-work round beads: white with pink rose, 6 mm
  - Czech glass hearts: light blue, 10 mm long
  - Czech glass leaves: light green, 12 mm long
  - Czech glass swirl beads: round, blue, 6 mm
  - Czech glass swirl beads: round, green, 6 mm
  - Czech glass swirl beads: round, pink, 6 mm
  - Fire-polished round Czech glass beads: amethyst, 6 mm
  - Fire-polished round Czech glass beads: green, 6 mm
  - Freshwater: rounded, flat-sided pearls, white, 5 mm
- Crimp beads: silver, 2
- Freshwater potato pearls: pale green, 8 mm, 4
- Freshwater rice pearls: white, 7 mm, 5
- Seed beads: pearlized, size 08, 18-25

MATERIALS
- Bead cord: elastic, 2' strand
- Bead wire: .012", 10" strand
- Head pins: silver, 36
- Pliers: chain nose, round nose, wire cutters
- Scissors
- Strong-hold glue

INSTRUCTIONS

To make button "beads": Choose eight pairs of buttons that match in diameter (colors can be different). Place them back to back, thread 3" strand of elastic bead cord through two of sew-through holes on one button, and up through the sew-through holes of top button.

Tie bead cord with surgeon's knot so two buttons fit together snugly. Apply dab of strong-hold glue to knot, let dry, and then trim ends of cord to knot. Repeat until you have eight button "beads."

To make bead dangles: String each of 36 assorted beads onto head pins. Turn ends of head pins into loops with pliers.

To assemble the bracelet: Thread about 2" of bead wire through two holes of remaining calico button. String crimp bead onto long end of wire and bring it to underside of button. Pass short end of wire through crimp bead also; crimp and trim. This button will form the closure for the bracelet.

String one 7 mm freshwater pearl onto bead wire, followed by four bead dangles from assortment of 36. String one button "bead" onto wire by pulling buttons apart slightly and inserting wire between them, being careful to place bead wire between two strands of elastic cord.

String another four bead dangles from assortment of 36 onto wire, followed by one 8 mm green potato pearl and another button "bead." Repeat this process until you have

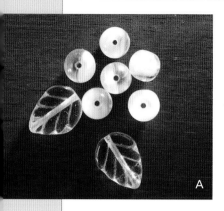

Photo A: The beads shown here are used in creating the earrings.

Below Right: To help the project go faster, make button "beads" ahead of time. If you prefer a contrasting-stitch look, use colored elastic bead cord.

Opposite Page: Calico buttons were essentially made using the same technique as transfer ware china—a piece of tissue paper was placed on a copper plate that had been etched with a pattern and then inked. The ink-printed tissue was then placed on the button blank and fired in a kiln, thereby transferring the pattern to the button.

used last button "bead," followed by last four bead dangles and last 7 mm freshwater pearl.

String crimp bead onto bead wire, followed by pearlized seed beads. Note: The number of seed beads is flexible because you will need to form them into a loop that fits comfortably over the button that you are using as a closure at the other end of the bracelet.

When you have gotten right number of seed beads, thread wire back through crimp bead and on through first few beads on bracelet. Use pliers to crimp; trim wire flush to one of bracelet beads.

Beaded Calico Button Earrings

BEADS & BUTTONS

- Antique calico china buttons: ⅝", 4
- Czech glass leaves: light green, 12 mm long, 2
- Czech glass swirl round beads: blue, 6 mm, 2
- Czech glass swirl round beads: green, 6 mm, 2
- Czech glass swirl round beads: pink, 6 mm, 2
- Freshwater pearls: rounded, flat-sided, white, 5 mm, 2
- Metal ball beads: silver, 2 mm, 2
- Spacer beads: daisy, silver, 4 mm, 2

MATERIALS
- Bead cord: elastic
- Eurowires (with loop): silver, 2
- Head pins: silver, 2
- Pliers: chain nose, round nose, wire cutters
- Strong-hold glue

INSTRUCTIONS

Make two button "beads" using four ⅝" calico buttons. Place them back to back, thread 3" strand of elastic bead cord through two of sew-through holes on one button, and up through sew-through holes of top button.

Tie bead cord with surgeon's knot so two buttons fit together snugly. Apply dab of strong-hold glue to knot, let dry, and then trim ends of cord to knot. Repeat until you have two button "beads."

Onto head pin, thread: one leaf bead, one pink, one blue, one green swirl bead drop, one 5 mm freshwater pearl bead drop, one button "bead," one spacer bead, and one 2 mm silver bead.

Form loop at top of head pin using pliers. Repeat to form second earring. Open loops on eurowires, attach bead/button dangle, and close loops.

A

China & Stencil Button Link Necklace & Earrings

When I was a small girl, my bedspread was a 1930s flower garden quilt pieced by my great-grandmother with the colorful flower-sack cottons of the day. These stencil buttons, contemporaries of the fabrics in my quilt, bring me the same sense of comfort and enjoyment as those whimsical cotton fabrics.

B

China & Stencil Button Link Necklace

BEADS & BUTTONS

- Aventurine beads: green, 10 mm, 21
- China and/or stencil buttons (circa 1920-30): ⅜"-⅝", 20

MATERIALS

- Eye pins: silver, 61
- Jump rings: silver, 4½ mm, 42
- Pliers: chain nose, round nose, wire cutters
- "S" hook and ring: silver

INSTRUCTIONS

Using two eye pins, wrap each china button to make it into necklace link. Use one eye pin with each aventurine bead to make bead links.

Join bead and button links with silver jump rings to form chain. Be careful to alternate button colors to achieve pleasing look.

Connect "S" hook to one end of necklace with jump ring. Connect silver ring to other end of necklace with jump ring.

Stencil Button Earrings

BEADS & BUTTONS

- Aventurine beads: green, 10 mm, 2
- China stencil buttons (can match or not): ⅝", 2

MATERIALS

- Eye pins: silver, 4
- French ear wires: silver, 2
- Head pins: silver, 2
- Scissors

INSTRUCTIONS

Using two eye pins, wrap each button and make into link. Insert head pins into aventurine beads; trim and turn to make loops.

Open loops on beads and attach them to bottom loops on buttons. Close loops.

Open loops on French wires and attach to top loops of buttons. Close French wire loops.

Photos A and B: The beads and buttons shown here are used in creating the necklace and earrings.

Right and Opposite Page: This necklace can be worn long or doubled. Use fewer buttons, beads, and jump rings if you prefer a shorter necklace. Make a few pairs of the earrings—one set from each type of button used to make the necklace. Old sewing chests provide great storage for button collections.

Stencil Button Bracelet

· ·

Anna Macedo created this bracelet to animate the delightful little designs of these glass stencil buttons from the 1920s. This piece is meant to slide over the hand, so you'll have to calculate how many rows of brick stitch it will take to make a band which will fit you.

Photo A: The beads and buttons shown here are used in creating the bracelet.

Opposite Page: The color of the beads perfectly accent the stencil buttons of this bracelet. You will want to bring your buttons with you when choosing beads for this project.

BEADS & BUTTONS
- Beads: bone-colored, 4 mm, 1 hank
- Beads: opaque Kelly green, 4 mm, 1 hank
- Beads: opaque yellow-orange, 5 mm, 1 strand
- Beads: iridescent glazed turquoise glass beads, #9, 1 hank
- Beads: iridescent glazed turquoise glass beads, #11, 1 strand
- Beads: white pearlized beads #9, 1 hank
- Glass seed beads: denim blue, #11, 1 hank
- Glass seed beads: opaque orange, #11, 1 hank
- Glass seed beads: translucent palest green, #11, 1 hank

MATERIALS
- Beading needle: #12
- Beading thread: style B, medium turquoise-colored, 1 spool
- Cuticle scissors

INSTRUCTIONS
Double Brick Stitch:

Row 1: String on 8 beads. (See Fig. A.)
Row 2: Turn and add 2 beads. Circle back through second bead and first bead of Row 1, and back through the first two beads of Row 2. (See Fig. B.) Pull up slack. The four beads will form a square, with two stacked on two. Add two more beads and circle through beads 3 and 4 of Row 1. Repeat. (See Fig. C.) This is a very strong weave, and an easy one to build. Stacked like bricks, one bead directly above another, the end product will look like this. (See Fig. D.)
Subsequent Rows: Continue to stack beads as shown. When you reach the end of your thread, weave ends back into the work and begin new thread by weaving up to your last bead worked.

DOUBLE BRICK STITCH

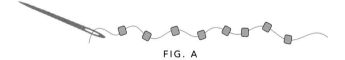

FIG. A

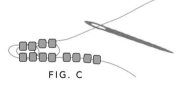

FIG. C

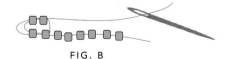

FIG. B

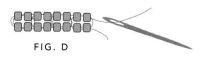

FIG. D

Hello

JAMES W. FOLEY

Brick stitch band: Begin Row 1 (string 8 beads). (See Fig. 1.) Double brick stitch for as many rows as necessary to create a bracelet that will slip on and off your hand. Keep your row count to an even number, as the motifs require multiples of four.

Bead and button fringe: Begin by weaving in thread, coming out on Row 2, between beads two and three. Attach fringe beads as shown (See Fig. 2), looping through last bead on fringe, and threading back through all beads. Repeat, for strength. Thread back into space between beads two and three, then come out between beads five and six. Repeat, skipping two beads in each row, and skipping one row of beads between each row of fringe motifs. (See Fig. 3.)

Here's how to alternate rows to make the buttons nicely spaced:

Row 1: button. (See Fig. 4.) Skip one row of beads.

Row 3: loop, yellow-orange bead, loop. (See Fig. 5.) Skip one row of beads.

Row 5: green bead, turquoise bead, green bead. (See Fig. 6.) Skip one row of beads. For the remaining rows, continue to alternate motifs in Rows 1 through 5. (See Fig. 7.) Remember to thread through each motif two times, for strength.

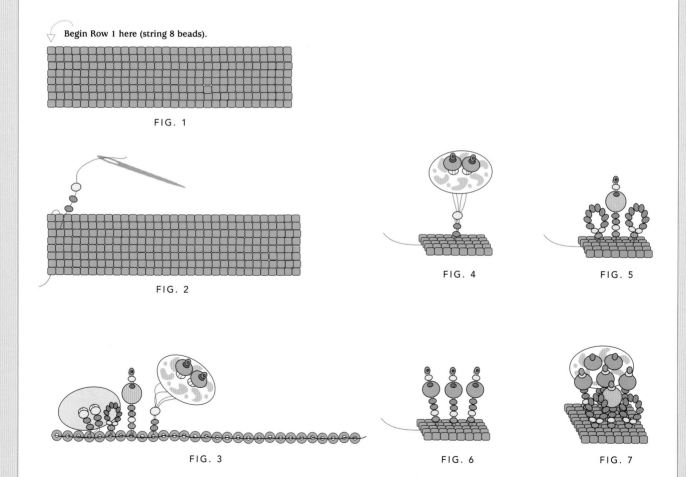

Begin Row 1 here (string 8 beads).

FIG. 1

FIG. 2

FIG. 3

FIG. 4

FIG. 5

FIG. 6

FIG. 7

A

Stacked Porcelain Button Brooches

For lovers of Victoriana, few buttons are as satisfying as these hand-painted floral porcelains. The backs of most of these buttons were marked with the initials of just such a young lady, identification for her buttons when they were sent off to the factory to be fired in a kiln.

Most of the porcelain pieces used here have shank button backs, which unfortunately are much harder to find than the more common porcelain studs. (These stud-backed buttons were used with blouses that had two rows of buttonholes down the front; the stud slipped through the holes much like a cuff link and could thus be worn interchangeably with various tops.)

Some especially large stone donuts have holes large enough to fit the porcelain stud; otherwise it is difficult to use these pieces without cutting the stud off.

Photo A: The beads and buttons shown here are used in creating the brooches.

Opposite Page: If you have trouble finding appropriate brass filigree stampings, try disassembling broken costume jewelry brooches or pendants.

BEADS & BUTTONS
- Donut spacer (slightly larger than porcelain button)
- Porcelain button: ¾"-1¼"

MATERIALS
- Filigree stamping (to be used as base or accent)
- Jewelry glue
- Pin back with bail

INSTRUCTIONS
Glue button to donut and donut to filigree piece. Let dry. Turn over and glue pin back with bail onto back. Let dry. Note: Some pieces shown follow a different order: button, filigree, stone donut.

BUTTON BASICS
Choosing Pieces For Your Brooch

The art to making these simple brooches is in choosing a button, filigree piece, and stone donut that complement one another in color and size. Other than that, making them is quite easy. The donut materials that seem to accent the floral porcelains best are yellow and olive jade, rose quartz, and mother-of-pearl. If you have difficulty finding new filigree stampings that please you, look for old pieces of costume jewelry that can be dismantled and the pin base reused.

BUTTON BASICS
Filigree Stampings Defined

Most jewelry findings are basically divided into two types: castings and stampings. Castings are thicker, three-dimensional findings made by either lost wax or centrifugal casting using models or molds. Stampings are one-sided pieces created when a thin sheet of metal is stamped between the male and female pieces of a die. Stampings were very popular in costume jewelry and button making in the late 19th and early 20th centuries. Many of the stampings available today are actually made in dies that were originally carved during those years. They are still used by the few stamping houses that remain in production today.

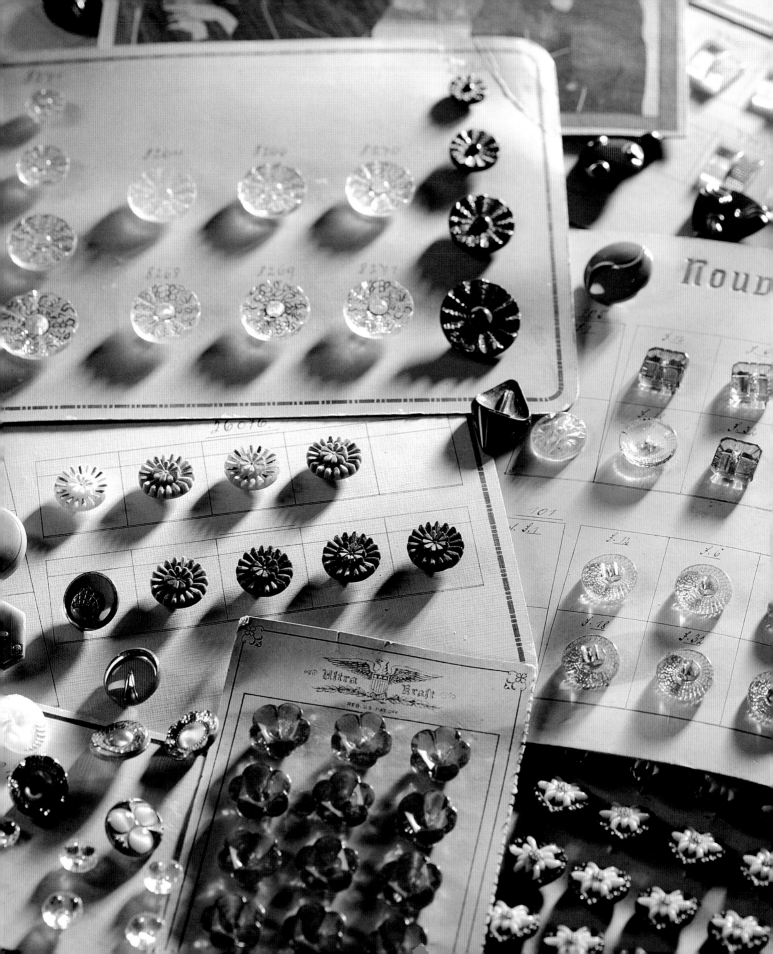

Chapter 6
Modern Glass Buttons

It is amazing that an item as small and seemingly insignificant as a button could be impacted in a major way by world events, but so it has always been with glass buttons. After World War II, a group of glass artisans from Bohemia fled across the Iron Curtain to establish a base in Bavaria, making Western Germany the glass button capital of the world for the next 20 years.

The methods they used were still very much the same as in the 19th century: Buttons were pressed in iron molds, trimmed and ground by hand, and polished in a tumbler. New techniques and paints made for some stunning changes and improvements, however, paint and metallic lusters had a more durable fired-on finish, and a method for mixing clear and opaque glass to form the cloud-like moonglow buttons was developed.

Moonglow buttons, such as the blue button found in our Anniversary Bracelet, are the most popular of all modern glass among button collectors. Collectors group them according to color—pinks, blues, greens, whites, and browns are the most common—and luster finish (silver or gold).

Glass "goofies" or "realistics" were also popular during this time. Sets of glass fruits and vegetables were produced in great quantities, as were sailboats, Scotty dogs, all varieties of hats and bonnets, and various flora and fauna. These buttons were whimsical in the extreme, and were often used on children's clothing.

As quickly as this passion for bright, cheerful, and beautiful glass buttons grew, it died in the mid-1960s. The sleek, zippered fashions of the day and the rapid spread of the automatic clothes washer and dryer marked the doom of the modern glass button. Or so it seemed at the time.

When the Iron Curtain fell in the 1990s, the newly formed Czech Republic opened up for trade again with the West. Button factories were given new life, antique molds were dusted off and put back into use. Today, dozens of small specialty button companies are importing buttons from the Czech Republic. These are available both through button distributors and on-line in a fascinating variety of colors, shapes, and subjects. They make for wonderful jewelry creating.

Anniversary Bracelet & Earrings

My parents were married in 1940, on the eve of World War II and just months after they had graduated from Louisiana State University with degrees in art. I made these porcelain and sterling photo charms using their senior year portraits and a wedding photo. The buttons reflect those popular during the early years of their marriage—crystal drops, rhinestones, and moonglows—plus a few china shoe buttons from my maternal grandmother's button box.

Photo A: The beads, buttons, charms, and chain shown here are used in creating the bracelet.

Opposite Page: Family memory or "scrapbook" button bracelets can be created for many occasions. They can be made for a mother using childhood pictures of her grown children and buttons from their baby clothes.

Anniversary Bracelet

BEADS & BUTTONS

- Spacer beads: daisy, antique silver, 4 mm, 4
- Vintage bead: oval, blue, and white striated, 18 mm long
- Vintage bead: oval, blue crystal, 16 mm long
- Vintage button: blue moonglow German glass, ¾"
- Vintage buttons: crystal, ⅜"-½", 4
- Vintage buttons: four-hole pearl shirt, ⅜", 3
- Vintage buttons: rhinestone, one blue, two crystal, ½"-¾"
- Vintage shoe buttons: white glass, ⅜", 2

MATERIALS

- Charm bracelet: silver, 7½" long (including ring and toggle)
- Epoxy glue
- Eye pins: silver, 6
- Filigree bead caps: antiqued silver, 2
- Head pins: silver, 3
- Jump rings: silver, 7 mm, 19
- Pliers: chain nose, round nose, wire cutters
- Porcelain photo charms, 3
- Toothpicks

INSTRUCTIONS

Assemble all charms. Turn sew-through pearls into charms using eye pins. Make bead charms by placing one spacer bead, one oval glass bead, one filigree bead cap, and one spacer bead on head pin. Make loop at top of head pin using pliers. Repeat with second oval glass bead.

Make charm with moonglow button by stringing it on head pin. Pull so end of head pin is lodged under button shank. Mix epoxy glue and place it over back of moonglow button. When glue is dry, use pliers to form head pin into loop at top of button. Trim and close loop.

Examine your crystal buttons. Those with wire shanks can be hung from bracelet with jump rings placed through shank. Those with self-shanks need to be wire wrapped with head pin using same process mentioned above for pearl buttons.

Place charm on every other link of bracelet, using jump rings, in this order: crystal button, small blue rhinestone button, pearl button, square charm, shoe button, crystal button, ¾" rhinestone button, blue crystal bead charm, pearl button, heart charm, crystal button, shoe button, moonglow button, pearl button, rhinestone button, round charm, blue striated oval bead, pearl button, crystal button.

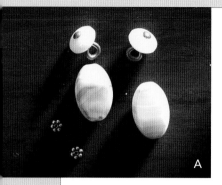

Photo A: The beads and buttons shown here are used in creating the Shoe Button & Vintage Bead Earrings.

Opposite Page: We were able to make both pairs of earrings shown here without damaging the shanks. With the rhinestone buttons, we simply folded the thin metal shanks against the base and glued the ear posts over them. With the beaded earrings, we used the shank of the shoe button as a loop from which to hang the bead dangle.

Rhinestone Button Clip-on Earrings

BEADS & BUTTONS
- Vintage crystal rhinestone buttons: blue, 1", 2

MATERIALS
- Glue-on earring posts and clutches
- Jewelry glue
- Nail file
- Pliers: cutter

INSTRUCTIONS
Using cutter pliers, snip off shanks of rhinestone buttons, smooth backs with nail file if necessary, and glue clips onto backs.

Note: Though we did not have to clip the shanks off of these particular rhinestone buttons to make these earrings, it may be necessary for you to do so with the ones you have found. This is especially not problematic if the buttons you are using are less than 20 years old and have thus not grown in value.

Shoe Button & Vintage Bead Earrings

BEADS & BUTTONS
- Vintage beads: oval, blue and white striated, 18 mm long, 2
- Vintage shoe buttons: white glass, 2

MATERIALS
- Eurowires: silver, 2
- Filigree bead caps: antique silver, 2
- Jump rings: silver oval, 5 x 7 mm, 2
- Pliers: chain nose

INSTRUCTIONS
Create bead dangle by stringing vintage oval bead, bead cap, and daisy spacer onto head pin. Use pliers to make loop at top of head pin.

Open loop of bead dangle and place over shank of shoe button. Close loop.

Open oval jump ring and thread it onto loop of eurowire. Slip opened oval jump ring around shank of shoe button and close it. Repeat all steps to make second earring.

West German Glass Button Bracelet & Earrings

Photos A and B: The beads and buttons shown here are used in creating the bracelet and earrings.

Opposite Page: Another charming version of this bracelet could be done with a pastel moonglow button and pastel glass beads.

One day in passing, I gave Joanna McLemore three of these vivid, 1950s West German painted glass paisley buttons. They were among the most striking of the painted buttons from that era I had ever seen. Her equally vivid imagination managed to turn those three buttons into this fanciful bracelet and earring set, which reminds me of retro, organic, and space-age design all at the same time.

West German Glass Button Bracelet

BEADS & BUTTONS
- Crimp beads: silver, 2
- Fire-polished Czech glass: diamond, hematite, 6 mm, 25
- Fire-polished Czech glass: round, hematite, 10 mm
- Seed beads: red, size 06, 74
- Vintage crackle glass nuggets: yellow, about 8 mm, 10
- Vintage jet painted glass button: red, yellow, blue, silver, ¾"

MATERIALS
- Bead wire: 30" strand
- Pliers: crimping
- Scissors

INSTRUCTIONS
Begin bracelet by stringing one crimp bead, two red seed beads, large hematite faceted round bead, and another red seed bead. Push end of bead wire back into large hematite bead, past single red seed bead, and continue to push bead wire into two red seed beads. Crimp bead. Note: There should be two "tails" of bead wire, one at ½" and remaining length. Secure crimp bead with crimping pliers.

String one diamond hematite glass bead, one red seed bead, one crackle glass nugget, and four more red seed beads onto two lengths of wire; shorter end should be completely covered.

Bring wire back through crackle glass nugget, pulling tight to create "loop" with four red seed beads.

String one diamond hematite, one red seed bead, one diamond hematite, one crackle glass nugget, and four red seed beads.

String wire back through crackle glass nugget, pulling tight to create "loop" with four red seed beads. Beaded section should look "V" shaped. Repeat until there are total of five crackle glass nuggets strung.

String one hematite bead and one red seed bead. Repeat four times until there is total of five hematite beads and five red seed beads.

Bring string back through the first two hematite beads and one seed bead. Pull tight and string button, then push string through fourth hematite bead, on side facing beaded section. Continue pushing wire through one red seed bead. Pull sting and make sure entire section is tight.

String one crackle glass bead and four red seed beads, bringing wire around and through crackle glass nugget, pulling tight to make "loop" with four red seed beads. Repeat process used on other side until there are five total crackle glass nuggets on each side of button.

String one hematite bead, one red seed bead, one hematite bead, one crimp bead, and 16 red seed beads and push wire through crimp bead, again making loop with 16 seed beads. Pull tight and make sure large hematite bead fits through loop and add or subtract red seed beads as necessary.

Opposite Page: You will have to experiment with how many red seed beads you need to form the loop closure on this bracelet; you want enough to fit comfortably around the end hematite bead, yet not so many that the closure is loose.

Continue pushing bead wire through last two hematite beads and one red seed bead and pull tight. Secure crimp bead with crimping pliers and cut excess wire close to second hematite bead wire was strung through.

West German Glass Button Earrings

BEADS & BUTTONS
- Fire-polished round Czech glass beads: hematite, 4 mm, 2
- Seed beads: red, size 06, 18
- Vintage crackle glass nuggets: yellow, about 8 mm, 2
- Vintage jet painted glass buttons: red, yellow, blue, silver, ¾", 2

MATERIALS
- Eye pins: silver, 4
- French ear wires (without loops): silver, 2
- Head pins: silver, 2
- Pliers: chain nose, round nose, wire cutters
- Strong-hold glue

INSTRUCTIONS

String four red seed beads onto eye pin. String one button onto same eye pin followed by four more red seed beads. Form loop at top of eye pin using pliers; cut excess wire.

String one vintage crackle glass nugget onto eye pin. Form loop at top of eye pin; attach to bottom of eye pin with button and close loop.

String one red seed bead onto head pin, form loop at top; attach to bottom of eye pin with crackle glass nugget and close.

Slip hematite bead onto unbent section of French wire, form loop, and attach to top of eye pin with button and close. Repeat to form second earring.

BUTTON BASICS
Positioning Earrings

To make sure the earrings hang correctly, you may want to turn them over, position ear wires in an upright position, and drop a little strong-hold glue along the sides of the seed beads. When this dries, it will keep the ear wire and button in the proper positions.

put buttons in here

HOLLYWOOD
REG. TRADE MARK

KY
CHARM
BUTTON
REG. APP. FOR

Presse
BUTTONS

Chapter 7
Bakelite & Celluloid Buttons

The word plastic comes from the Greek word plastikos, which means "to retain a shape when molded." Using this sense of the word, the earliest plastics used to make buttons were these natural materials—horn, tortoise shell, and vulcanized rubber—which could be heated and pressed into molds. But by today's meaning, plastic substances are synthetic or at least semi-synthetic materials that can be molded with the application of pressure or heat. The earliest types of plastics used to make buttons were celluloid and Bakelite. All but the most involved button cognoscenti constantly misidentify celluloid buttons as the (usually) more desirable Bakelite.

Celluloid, the first man-made plastic, was developed in England in the 1850s but not employed commercially until 1868, when John Wesley Hyatt of Newark, New Jersey attempted to make simulated ivory billiard balls with it. A popular button material from the 1870s through the 1930s, celluloid is actually a combination of cellulose (plant fiber), nitric and sulfuric acids, and camphor. It is lighter and more brittle than Bakelite, and has the flaw of being extremely flammable (celluloid film caused more than one disastrous fire in early movie theaters before it was replaced by the more stable cellulose acetate).

Our favorite celluloid buttons are the large, flat, layered, and carved coat buttons from the 1920s called "wafers." Because of their striking linear Art Deco carvings, these buttons are more frequently than not misidentified as Bakelite.

Bakelite was the first entirely synthetic, man-made plastic. It was discovered in 1909 when successful Belgian chemist Leo Baekeland (he had invented Velux photo paper) combined phenol (carbolic acid) with formaldehyde in a test tube in an attempt to create a synthetic shellac in his Yonkers, New York laboratory. Far from creating shellac, this combination became rock hard and was impervious to solvents and could not be heated and remolded. Thus Bakelite was also the first thermosetting plastic (as opposed to the thermoplastic substances like celluloid and caesin, which can be heated and remolded).

Bakelite Babies

• •

Celeste Layrisson, a Louisiana antique dealer and part-time button collector, developed her own method for creating these "Bakelite Babies" years ago. These samples from her private collection can be adapted to hang as pendants on black necklace cords. Note the "baby" with the star badge and hat—Celeste's husband is a retired sheriff.

Photo A: The beads and buttons shown here are used in creating the Bakelite Babies.

Above: Use theme buttons to personalize the Bakelite Babies for gift giving.

Opposite Page: Search for broken Bakelite necklaces and bracelets to find the beads to make these "babies."

BEADS & BUTTONS
• Bakelite bead: green, ¾"
• Bakelite bead: yellow, ⅞"
• Bakelite beads: clear yellow, ½", 2
• Bakelite beads: green, ⅜", 2
• Bakelite beads: orange, ⅜", 2
• Bakelite beads: red, ⅜", 2
• Bakelite cone button: yellow, ½"
• Bakelite "gear" button: maroon, ⅝"
• Bakelite "gear" buttons: green, ½", 2
• Bakelite "gear" buttons: orange, ⁵/₁₆", 2
• Bakelite "gear" buttons: yellow, ½", 2
• Bakelite ruffled button: green, 1½"

MATERIALS
• Black elastic cording: 8" length
• Black elastic cording: 22" length
• Celluloid purse charm
• Drill press
• Matches
• Necklace cord: 24" length
• Scissors

INSTRUCTIONS
Create body for Bakelite Baby by drilling second hole in ⅞" yellow bead. Drill this hole at right angle to existing bead hole, placing it slightly above center of bead to give arms right position. (The original bead hole may also have to be re-drilled to make it big enough for the elastic cording to pass through. Use a drill bit large enough to do this for both holes. Also, always wear a mask covering your nose and mouth when drilling Bakelite as the Bakelite dust can be harmful.)

Fold 22"-long piece of elastic cording in half; make small loop (about ¼") and knot at folded end.

To create hat, run both ends of folded cording through shank of cone button and through two sew-through holes of maroon gear button. Next, ¾" green bead will be threaded for head. Orange "gear" button will be added next for the collar. Then run both ends of cord through middle hole in ⅞" yellow bead. When two ends of cord come out of bottom of ⅞" bead, thread them through two sew-through holes in 1½" ruffled Bakelite button to make skirt.

Make legs by threading one ½" clear yellow bead, one ½" green "gear" button, and one ⅜" red bead onto each strand of elastic. Finish legs by making knot in cording immediately under red beads, trimming and then sealing by holding lit match for just a second to cording to melt and seal the end.

Thread second, shorter piece of elastic cording through hole drilled for arms of "baby." Pull it so equal lengths of elastic are on each side. On each side, beginning at yellow "body" bead, string one ½" yellow "gear" button, one ⅜" green bead, and one ⁵/₁₆" orange bead. On right side, string purse charm on elastic after orange bead. Tie off both ends of cording and singe as done above.

A

B

Photos A and B: The beads and buttons shown here are used in creating the bracelet and earrings.

Below and Opposite Page: A much easier version of the crocheted button bracelet, this statement-making bracelet is made by simply sewing buttons onto a length of elastic. For a different look, the bracelet and earrings can also be designed with colorful glass buttons.

Bakelite Button Elastic Bracelet & Earrings

This bracelet is sort of a cheater's version of the Crocheted Button Bracelet in Chapter 3. While it is easy to sew the layered Bakelite buttons onto the elastic band, it is hard is to let go of so many of your favorite Bakelite buttons to make just one piece of jewelry.

Bakelite Button Elastic Bracelet

BEADS & BUTTONS
- Bakelite buttons: ⅞"-1⅜", 20
- Bakelite buttons: ¼"-¾", 16

MATERIALS
- Elastic banding: black, heavy, 1" wide, 8" length
- Needle
- Scissors
- Thread: black, heavy, 1 spool

INSTRUCTIONS
Form bracelet band by overlapping elastic (turning under ends for neat finish) and sewing closed to form 6½" ring.

Sew two overlapping rows of larger Bakelite buttons onto elastic, adding smaller Bakelite button to top of any larger button that is sew-through. Note: On our bracelet, we have four larger buttons that are not sew-through and that stand on their own—three squared box buttons and one lattice square button.

Tie off thread when finished with each row. Distribute buttons with eye toward pleasing color and shape combinations.

Bakelite Ball Earrings

BEADS & BUTTONS
- Glass round beads: black, 6 mm, 2
- Glass round beads: cherry red, 4 mm, 2
- Glass round beads: jade green, 4 mm, 2
- Glass round beads: jade green, 6 mm, 2
- Glass round beads: translucent yellow, 4 mm, 2
- Vintage Bakelite ball buttons: cherry red, 2

MATERIALS
- Eye pins: silver, 2
- French ear wire: silver, 2
- Head pins: silver, 10
- Pliers: chain nose, round nose, wire cutters

INSTRUCTIONS
Turn each Bakelite ball into dangle by threading long silver eye pin through button shank, so about ¾ of pin nearest eye is one side of shank.

Bend eye up and back so it is positioned directly over sew-through shank. Take other end of pin and wrap it around eye end. Trim excess wire.

Thread each bead onto head pin and turn into dangle with pliers. Trim excess wire.

Attach French wires to loop at top of Bakelite ball. Attach one of each color bead to "stem" formed by wire wrapping above each Bakelite ball.

Bakelite & Coral Necklace & Earrings

Any fan of Bakelite has accumulated a number of single carved buckle halves and large, chunky coat buttons. While wonderful to look at, these pieces can be difficult to wear and enjoy today. We've come up with an unbelievably simple method for transforming these pieces into interchangeable pendants to wear with a strand of coral beads, a method that doesn't harm the buckle or button at all.

Photos A and B: The beads and buttons shown here are used in creating the necklace and earrings.

Opposite Page: Unlike later plastics that were molded, Bakelite had to be carved by hand using a press or wheel, a technique that gives it its primitive, almost ethnic look. Pendants are easily changed out with the addition of "S" hooks.

Bakelite & Coral Necklace

BEADS & BUTTONS
- Bakelite buckle halves or buttons with 2 loop shanks: large, 1 or more
- Bamboo coral beads: red, 16 mm, 16" strand
- Crimp beads: silver, 2

MATERIALS
- Bead wire: .018", 20" length
- Fold-over bracelet links: silver, 2 or more
- Jump rings: sterling silver, 2
- Pliers: crimping
- "S" hooks: sterling silver, 3
- Scissors

INSTRUCTIONS
Make finished necklace with bamboo coral by stringing beads on bead wire and finishing ends with crimp beads, jump rings, and "S" hooks.

To make button drops: Open one end of "S" hook and thread it through double loop shanks of button. Squeeze closed. To wear, place other end of "S" hook between middle beads of coral necklace and squeeze closed. Button should hang nicely on beads and "S" hook should be barely visible.

To make buckle drops: Place two fold-over bracelet links in middle of metal bar on back of buckle, leaving ⅛" open between them. Squeeze them shut so they stay in place on bar.

Open both ends of their "S" hook. Thread one end of "S" hook over bar on buckle, between two fold-over bracelet links. Twist or squeeze shut. This drop can also be worn on the coral necklace by placing other end of "S" hook between middle beads of necklace.

BUTTON BASICS
The Cost of Bakelite

Prices for Bakelite have skyrocketed in the past 10 years. Desirable brooches and bracelets routinely sell for several hundreds of dollars, while sought-after figural buttons are usually priced at $50 to $100 or more. With that in mind, it is easy to see how one of the most affordable ways to enjoy Bakelite is to salvage orphaned buckle halves or fairly common coat buttons as shown here.

Opposite Page: We have
made several earrings using
this technique: placing an
eye pin through the shank
of a button and filling up
the blank space on the pin
with seed beads. It is always
necessary to secure the pin
to the inside of the beads
and the beads to the back
of the button with strong-
hold glue. Otherwise the
button will spin around
on the pin and not hang
correctly. When making the
pendant—if you are using
a button with a single shank
(some were so heavy they
had two shanks), don't
worry that your pendant
looks as if it won't hang
correctly. When placed
against your chest it will
sit the right way.

Bakelite & Coral Earrings

BEADS & BUTTONS

- Red bamboo coral beads: 14 mm, 2
- Seed beads: red, size 06, 16
- Vintage Bakelite buttons in matching color: 1", 2

MATERIALS

- Eye pins: silver, 2
- French ear wires: silver, 2
- Head pins: silver, 2
- Pliers: chain nose, round nose, wire cutters
- Strong-hold glue

INSTRUCTIONS

Thread four red seed beads onto eye pin, followed by button shank and four more seed beads. Form loop at top of head pin with pliers. Attach ear wire to this loop.

Turn red bamboo coral beads into charms with head pins. Attach to bottom loop of eye pin. Repeat to form second earring.

Note: To make sure earrings hang correctly, you may want to turn them over, position ear wires in upright position, and put a few drops of strong-hold glue on seed beads and button shanks where the eye pins pass through. When this dries, it will keep ear wire and button in proper positions.

BUTTON BASICS
Adding Buckle Drops

You can make as many similar Bakelite drops as you wish for your coral necklace. Simply bend the top end of the "S" hook open gently to slide each drop off and put another one on. This is a wonderful way to use and enjoy more affordable Bakelite pieces (i.e., single buckle halves and basic black carved coat button) that are relatively easy to find and won't break the bank as will a rare, carved figural pin or pendant.

125

Stacked Celluloid Button Brooches

Nowhere does the stacking method of button jewelry making produce more dramatic results than with these celluloid coat buttons from the 1920s and '30s. The geometric nature of their Art Deco designs makes them naturals for stacking and contrasting pattern to pattern, color to color. These brooches, formed with a base of one or two celluloid buttons and centered with a variety of buttons or cabochons, have a look that is both ethnic and retro, sophisticated and funky.

BEADS & BUTTONS

- Vintage button, glass, or stone cabochon (for center element)
- Vintage celluloid button: ¾"-1¼"
- Vintage celluloid or Bakelite button: 1¼"-2"

MATERIALS

- Jewelry glue
- Pin back: glue-on with bail

INSTRUCTIONS

Stack two buttons and cabochon, one on top of the other, then glue. Let dry. Turn brooch over and glue pin back in middle of top half of back of largest celluloid button.

Photo A: The beads and buttons shown here are used in creating the brooch.

Above: Use a pin back or a pin back with a bail—the choice is up to you.

Opposite Page: Note the button card on the left side; the illustration shows just the kind of 1920s coat these celluloid buttons were used on. When shopping in vintage stores, remember to look on the clothing for unique and sometimes valuable button finds.

BUTTON BASICS
Identifying Celluloid Buttons

For years, button collectors recommended testing for celluloid by heating a needle with a flame, and gently pricking the back of the button. If the needle went in easily, then the button was probably celluloid. This is seldom recommended today, as at the very least it damages the back of the button and, at the worst, it can make your easily flammable celluloid piece burst into flames. A safer test is to microwave a cup of water on high for one minute. Dip an inconspicuous edge of the button into the water for just three seconds. Lift the piece to your nose and sniff; if there is a whiff of camphor (like Vicks Vapor Rub), then the button is celluloid.

BUTTON BASICS
Caring for Celluloid Buttons

Store your celluloid buttons in a container with airflow. When celluloid is stored with metal in an airtight container (such as a button tin), a chemical reaction is triggered, which causes deterioration of both the celluloid and the metal.

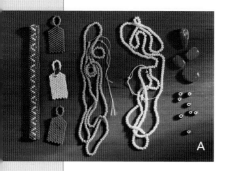

Back to School -1957 Necklace

Made by Anna Macedo, this red plaid amulet bag necklace with celluloid leaf button was inspired by a wonderful celluloid button she discovered. The lines and playful spirit of this red leaf reminded her of the little school dresses worn in the late 50s. She particularly remembered having a collection of bright plaid frocks with decorative buttons and pristine little white collars. Anna had great fun inventing a colorful plaid pattern in the peyote stitch and creating a necklace that showcases this marvelous button.

Photo A: The beads and buttons shown here are used in creating the necklace.

Opposite Page: The plaid pattern of the bag is reminiscent of school-girl uniforms. Though we used a vintage button, there are modern buttons available that would work just as well.

BEADS & BUTTONS
- Delica beads: 1 small bag each
  - #791 red (matte, opaque)
  - #751 yellow (matte, opaque)
  - #756 blue (matte, opaque)
  - #200 white (glossy, opaque)
  - #655 green (glossy, opaque)
  - #182 gray (opaque)
- Glass seed beads: #11, light green, 1 hank
- Glass teardrop beads: cobalt blue, 13
- Glass tubular beads: red, 11
- Opaque glass bead: light green, 6 mm
- Pearlescent glass seed beads: #11, yellow, 1 strand
- Translucent glass beads: cobalt blue, 4 mm, 23
- Vintage celluloid leaf button: red

MATERIALS
- #12 beading needle
- Beading thread: bright red, style B, 1 spool
- Cuticle scissors

INSTRUCTIONS
See diagrams on page 131.

Basic Peyote Stitch:

Row 1: String on six beads. (See Fig. A.)

Row 2: Turn and add green bead. Go through second bead of Row 1. Skip red bead and add another green bead, going through second green bead on Row 1. Add last green bead as shown. (See Fig. B.) Pull up slack so each green bead sits on top red bead in Row 1. Row 2 is now made. (See Fig. C.)

Row 3: Turn and add red bead. Go through green bead, which sits high, inviting you to string through it. Repeat, adding one red bead between each green bead in Row 2. Row 3 is finished. (See Fig. D.)

Subsequent Rows: Continue alternating colors and stacking beads as shown. You will be creating a mosaic of beads. (See Fig. 1.) When you reach end of thread, weave ends back into work and secure new thread by weaving up to last bead worked.

Amulet Bag: Thread needle with comfortable length of thread. String on 40 delica beads in alternating colors according to pattern. Using basic peyote stitch, follow pattern for 30 rows, until one panel is completed. Begin second panel in same fashion and follow pattern to completion.

Weave panels together at sides and bottom, creating vertical rectangular bag. (See Fig. 2.) Note: Because the piece is rectangular and not square (a mathematical detail), the plaid will not match precisely at the seams. This is not noticeable when the piece is finished.

Necklace Strap: To begin Row 1, string six beads: one blue, four reds, one blue. Using basic peyote stitch, repeat motifs until necklace is as long as you like. Remember to end with four rows of red and blue beads, just like in first four rows. The necklace strap featured here has 76 motifs, plus four rows of red and blue beads at each end.

Top and Above: The school-girl plaid of the amulet bag is perfectly accented by the red arrowhead button. The button is attached to the back of the bag and drapes over the front.

Attaching Strap: Sew strap to back panel only by weaving thread through several rows of beads, in and around, until straps are secure. (See Fig. 3.) Make every effort to conceal thread.

Adding Embellishments: To front panel only, attach 11 evenly spaced sets of trim beads by weaving thread in and around several rows of beads. (See Fig. 4.) Trim will stand up in front of straps and across front panel. Add 11 sets of trim to bottom seam by using same method of weaving. Be careful to conceal thread for clean, finished look.

Adding Button Closure: From back panel, count 14 rows from top and seven beads from left edge. (See Fig. 5.) This is where thread should emerge to begin closure. String on 22 #11 green beads, one large green bead, and 12 #11 green beads. Go through second hole of leaf button, string on cobalt bead, go back through three green #11 beads, and up through first hole in button.

Add cobalt bead and secure both cobalt beads by repeatedly going through button-holes and three green beads at back. Come back out second cobalt bead, string on seven #11 green beads, and go back through large green bead. Add 22 green #11 beads to finish closure, and weave into amulet bag in same row you came out of, but 14 beads to right. Pass through entire closure once or twice to strengthen it.

Secure thread by weaving around inside peyote stitch of back panel. Closure should slip between trim beads at front of bag, and easily fold over top edge of bag.

Adding Fringe: There are 11 strands of beaded fringe, strung as shown, through the 11 red beads. (See Fig. 6.)

Strand 1: String 14 green beads, 1 yellow bead, 1 red oval bead, 1 yellow bead, 10 green beads, 1 yellow bead, 1 cobalt drop, 1 yellow bead, 9 green beads, 14 green beads.

Strand 2: String 16 green beads, *1 yellow bead, 1 red oval bead, 1 yellow bead, 10 green beads, 1 yellow bead, 1 cobalt drop, 1 yellow bead, 9 green beads*, 16 green beads.

Strand 3: String 18 green beads and repeat * to *.

Strand 4: String 20 green beads and repeat * to *.

Strand 5: String 22 green beads and repeat * to *.

Strand 6: String 24 green beads and repeat * to *.

Strand 7: String 22 green beads and repeat * to *.

Strand 8: String 20 green beads and repeat * to *.

Strand 9: String 18 green beads and repeat * to *.

Strand 10: String 16 green beads and repeat * to *.

Strand 11: String 14 green beads and repeat * to *.

Examine necklace for errant thread ends. Snip loose threads or fibers closely with cuticle scissors. Gently polish with clean, slightly damp cloth to remove any mild residue.

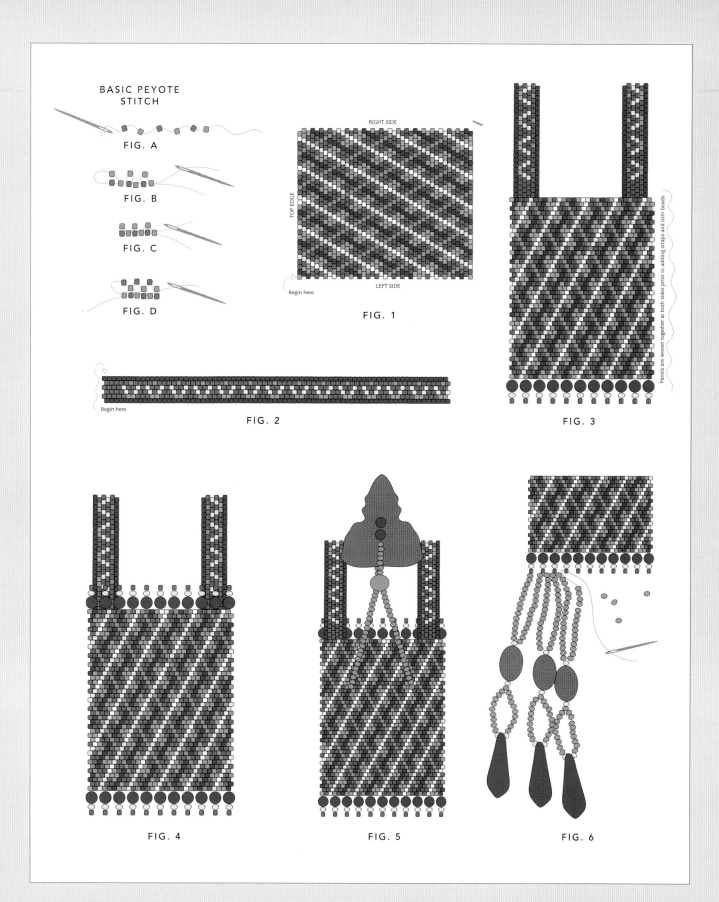

BASIC PEYOTE
STITCH

FIG. A

FIG. B

FIG. C

FIG. D

FIG. 1

RIGHT SIDE

TOP EDGE

LEFT SIDE

Begin here.

FIG. 2

Begin here.

FIG. 3

Panels are woven together at both sides prior to adding straps and trim beads.

FIG. 4

FIG. 5

FIG. 6

Anna's Folly Necklace

With this necklace, Anna Macedo challenged herself to create a whimsical necklace using two rather plain vintage buttons from my collection. It occurred to her that these unassuming celluloid buttons might have more appeal when stacked. She spiced them up by threading with a contrasting color. Raiding her stash of miscellaneous glass beads of all shapes and sizes, she chose the best of the primary colors. She enjoys the counterpoint of matte and glossy beads together, so she experimented with this, deciding upon the double peyote stitch for the pouch. The result was a colorful amulet bag necklace with stacked celluloid buttons that wears well with denim or a simple sundress.

Photo A: The beads and buttons shown here are used in creating the necklace.

Opposite Page: Two rather plain buttons set the stage for the primary colors chosen to complete this amulet bag. The bag is made using a double peyote beading stitch, but the strap was simply strung with beads.

BEADS & BUTTONS
- Assorted beads: disks, waters, barrels, ovals, melons, or other interesting, primary colored glass beads, in even numbers, 20-30
- Delica beads: 1 small bag each
  -#791 red (matte, opaque)
  -#277 cobalt blue (glossy, translucent)
- Glass beads: cobalt blue translucent, 4 mm, 1 hank
- Glass beads: light green translucent, 7 mm, 4
- Glass beads: red opaque, 5 mm, 1 strand
- Glass beads: yellow translucent, 4 mm, 1 hank
- Glass seed beads: #11, orange opaque, 1 hank
- Glass tubular beads: red, 4
- Glass teardrop beads: cobalt blue, 6
- Vintage celluloid coat buttons: green, 2

MATERIALS
- Beading needle: #12
- Beading thread: style B, bright red, 1 spool
- Cuticle scissors

INSTRUCTIONS
See diagrams on page 135.

Double Peyote Stitch:

Row 1: String on 64 beads, alternating two reds and two blues. (See Fig. 1.)

Row 2: Turn and add two red beads. Go through third and fourth beads of Row 1. Add two red beads, going through sixth and seventh beads on Row 1. (See Fig. 2.) Pull up slack so each red bead sits atop red bead in Row 1. Row 2 is now made. (See Fig. 3.)

Row 3: Turn and add two red beads. Repeat, adding a pair of red beads between each two beads in Row 2. Row 3 is finished. (Fig. 4)

Subsequent Rows: Continue alternating colors and stacking beads as shown. (See Fig. 5.) You will be creating a mosaic of beads (See Fig. 6.) When you reach end of thread, weave ends back into work. Trim thread ends closely. Secure new thread by weaving up through few rows and out of last bead worked.

Amulet Bag: Thread needle with comfortable length of thread. String on 64 delica beads in alternating colors, according to pattern. (See Fig. 7.) Using double peyote stitch, follow pattern for 48 rows. Fold piece in half and weave panels together at side and bottom, creating square pouch.

Flap: Weave in long thread and emerge from top edge of pouch. Skip first pair of beads in row, and double peyote stitch across edge (seven pairs of beads across). Leave one space left over at edge. (See Fig. 8.) Continue double peyote stitch for 40 rows; weave thread and trim off. Stack buttons and sew into middle of flap, making sure buttons show when flap is folded over front of pouch.

Adding Embellishments: To each side of pouch, attach 10 evenly spaced sets of trim beads by weaving thread in and around several rows of beads. (See Fig. 9.) Trim should stand up nicely. Add seven sets of trim to bottom seam by using same method of weaving. Add your choice of glass bead fringes to each trim, and be sure to weave thread through fringes several times for strength. Conceal thread for clean, finished look.

Necklace Strap: Anchor very long thread into pouch, emerging from top edge. (See Fig. 9.) String double loop of orange and blue beads and culminate these into single green anchor bead, as shown. Add variety of accent beads for few inches, then alternate 5 mm red and 5 mm blue beads for remainder of necklace. Repeat accent beads at other end, and weave thread through entire necklace several times for strength. Anchor thread and trim any loose ends with cuticle scissors.

Examine your necklace for errant thread ends. Snip loose threads or fibers closely with cuticle scissors. Gently polish with clean, slightly damp cloth to remove any mild residue.

Right: We stacked two green buttons for the bag—contrasting buttons would also work well here.

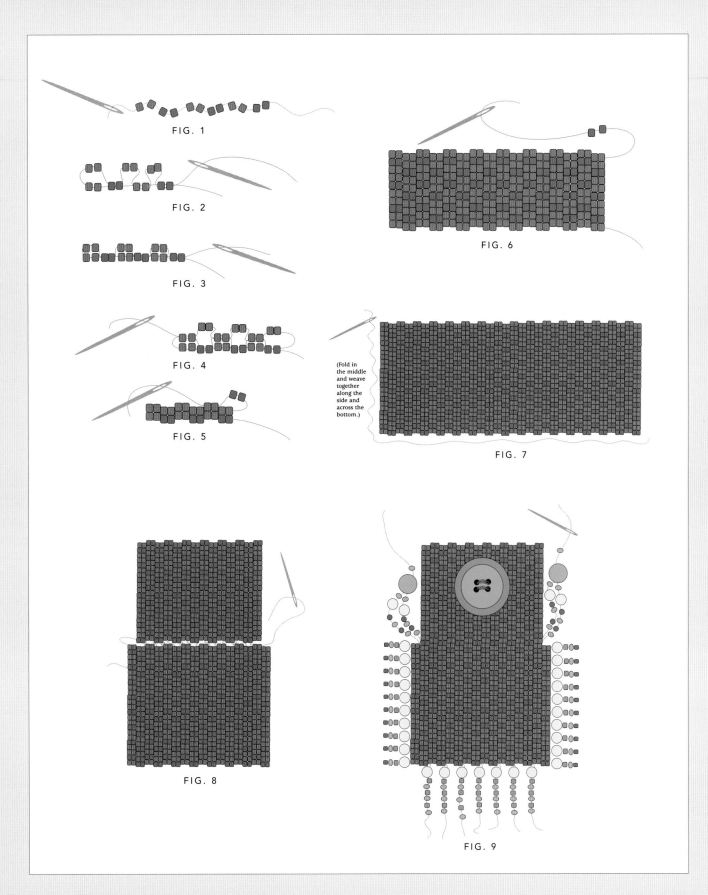

FIG. 1

FIG. 2

FIG. 3

FIG. 4

FIG. 5

FIG. 6

(Fold in the middle and weave together along the side and across the bottom.)

FIG. 7

FIG. 8

FIG. 9

Gumdrop Bracelet

Photo A: The beads and buttons shown here are used in creating the bracelet.

Opposite Page: Created using techniques also found in the Stencil Button Bracelet, our Gumdrop Bracelet makes a bold statement with stacked Bakelite buttons.

Another beaded fringe bracelet from Anna Macedo. This piece was inspired by this great red and black Bakelite button, which reminded Anna of a cherry gumdrop. This bracelet has lots of fringe and smaller elements, so it's deliciously tactile on the wrist. You'll recognize some of the same basic instructions from the Stencil Button Bracelet.

This bracelet is meant to slide over the hand, so you'll have to calculate how many rows of brick stitch it will take to make a band that will fit you. It takes some planning and a bit of math to work out the numbers of rows of fringe motifs. For this bracelet, there are three repeating rows of motifs, plus another 10 rows, and the button—that's 11 rows plus a multiple of three. Of course the pattern can be altered to accommodate a clasp, if you desire, but I prefer the decadent richness of an unbroken carpet of fringe.

BEADS & BUTTONS
- Matte black leaf beads: ½" long, 10
- Opaque glass round beads: black, 4 mm, 1 hank
- Opaque glass round beads: bright orange, 4mm, 1 hank
- Opaque glass beads: green, #8, 1 hank
- Seed beads: black opaque glass #11, 1 hank
- Seed beads: bright orange glass, #11, 1 hank
- Seed beads: bright red glass, #11, 1 hank
- Seed beads: medium blue glass, #11, 1 hank
- Seed beads: sky blue glass, #11, 1 hank
- Seed beads: yellow pearlized glass, #11, 1 hank
- Vintage red glass flat triangle beads, 1 small bag

MATERIALS
- Beading needle: #12
- Beading thread: style B medium, green, 1 spool
- Cuticle scissors

INSTRUCTIONS
See diagrams on page 139.

Double brick stitch:

Row 1: String on 8 beads. (See Fig. A.)

Row 2: Turn and add two beads. Circle back through second bead and first bead of Row 1, and back through the first two beads of Row 2. (See Fig. B.) Pull up slack. The four beads will form a square, with two stacked on two. Add two more beads and circle through beads three and four of Row 1. Repeat. (See Fig. C.) This is a very strong weave, and an easy one to build. Stacked like bricks, one bead directly above another, the end product will look like this. (See Fig. D.) *Subsequent Rows:* Continue to stack beads as shown. When you reach the end of your thread, weave ends back into the work and begin new thread by weaving up to your last bead worked.

Brick stitch band: Begin Row 1 (See Fig. 1.) string eight beads. Double brick stitch, using green #8 beads, for as many rows as necessary to create a bracelet that will slip on and off over your hand. Keep your row count to an odd number, as the motifs require 11 rows plus a multiple of three.

Button Centerpiece: Sew your button securely into one row of beaded band, going through three or four beads in two rows several times. String length of new thread. Secure your thread by repeatedly going through the beads in the first two rows from button's center. Skip two rows and begin your first row of fringe, emerging just under edge of button for lushly fringed appearance.

Beaded fringe: Begin by weaving in thread just under button, coming out of beaded band at Row 3 from center of button, between beads two and three (See Fig. 2.). We will call this row Fringe Row 1.

Above: We stacked two whimsical buttons to create the focus of the bracelet. The red button reminded Anna of a gumdrop and was the inspiration for the name.

Fringe Row 1: Attach fringe beads as shown (see Fig. 3a.)—one #11 yellow, four #11 sky blues, one #8 green, one red triangle, one #11 medium blue. Loop through last bead on fringe, and thread back into red triangle and through all beads. Thread through once again, for strength. Thread back into band in space between beads two and three, then come out between beads four and five. Repeat motif. Skip two beads, coming out between beads six and seven. Repeat motif.

Fringe Row 2 (See Fig. 3b.): Skip first two beads in next row, come out between beads two and three. Make loop of beads to support your first leaf bead, by stringing one #11 yellow, four #11 medium blue, one #11 red, one black leaf bead, one #11 red, four #11 medium blues, and thread back through yellow bead and into band. Thread through motif once again, for strength. Thread back into band in space between beads two and three, then come out between beads six and seven. Repeat motif with loop and leaf bead. There are only two motifs—each with one leaf bead—in this row.

Fringe Row 3 (See Fig. 3c.): Next row, skip first two beads and come out between beads two and three. String one #11 yellow, four #11 sky blues, one #8 green, one 4 mm black bead, and one #11 orange bead. Go back through black bead and down through all beads in motif. Thread through all again for strength. Skip two beads, coming out between beads four and five. Repeat motif. Skip two beads, coming out between beads six and seven. Repeat motif.

Fringe Row 4 (See Fig. 3a.): Repeat Row 1.

Fringe Row 5 (See Fig 3b.): There will be three leaf motifs in this row. Skip first two beads and come out between beads two and three. Make loop of beads to support your first leaf bead, by stringing one #11 yellow, four #11 medium blue, one #11 red, one black leaf bead, one #11 red, four #11 medium blues, and thread back through yellow bead and into band. Thread through motif once again, for strength. Thread back into band in space between beads two and three, then come out between beads four and five. Repeat motif with loop and leaf bead. Thread back into band in the space between beads four and five, then come out between beads six and seven. Repeat motif.

Fringe Row 6 (See Fig. 3c.): Repeat Row 3. Now we've begun our three alternating rows of motifs which will be repeated around band until we're within five rows of spot where button is attached.

Fringe Row 7 (See Fig. 3d): Skip first two beads and come out between beads two and three. String on one #11 yellow, four #11 reds, one #11 yellow, one 3mm orange, 1 #11 black. Go back through orange bead and down through all beads in motif. Thread through all again for strength. Skip two beads, coming out between beads four and five. Repeat motif. Skip two beads, coming out between beads six and seven. Repeat motif.

Subsequent Rows: Repeat Row 1, Row 3, and Row 7 (Fig. 3a, 3c & 3d), alternating these rows all around your band until you come within five rows of where button is attached. Repeat Row 5 (the three-leaf row), Row 4 (a triangle row), Row 3 (a black bead row), Row 2 (a two-leaf row), and Row 1 (a triangle row).

When all rows are completed, I like to thread back and fourth through the entire band again (just the green beaded band, not the fringe motifs), to pull up any slack and straighten up my rows. This bracelet is pleasantly flexible, but sturdy enough to last for many years.

Finish: Examine your necklace for errant thread ends. Snip loose threads or fibers closely with cuticle scissors.

DOUBLE BRICK STITCH

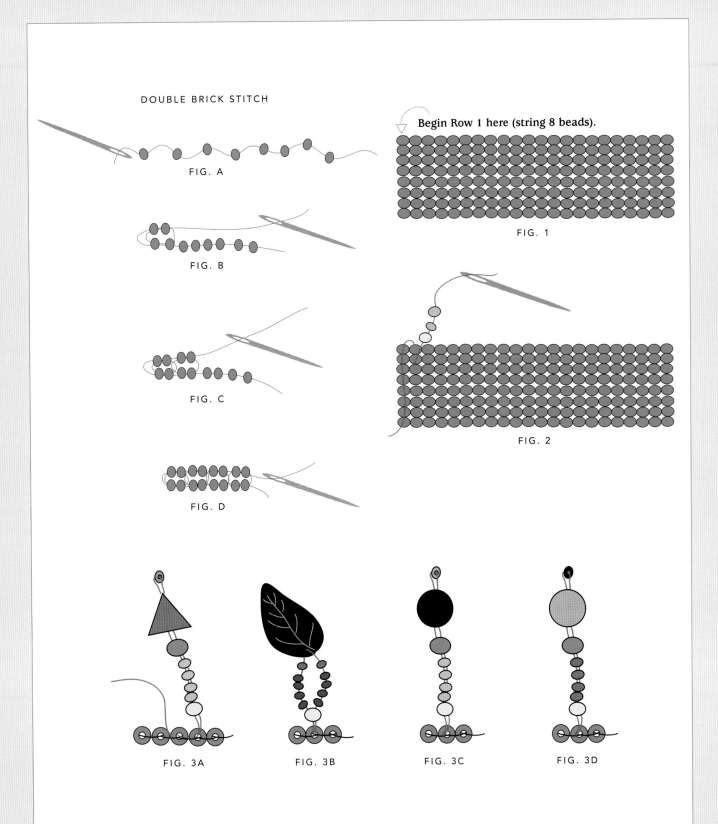

FIG. A

FIG. B

FIG. C

FIG. D

Begin Row 1 here (string 8 beads).

FIG. 1

FIG. 2

FIG. 3A

FIG. 3B

FIG. 3C

FIG. 3D

ABOUT THE AUTHOR

As the youngest of four sisters reared in rural historic St. Francisville, Louisiana, Susan Davis learned to love both art and history at an early age. Her childhood (and current) hometown fits William Faulkner's description of a place where "the past isn't dead, it isn't even past." Susan and her friends hunted Easter eggs among the moss-covered tombstones of the town's antebellum cemetery and built playhouses in the crumbling, overgrown garden structures of 19th-century mansions.

Though neither of Susan's parents pursued careers as artists, they both graduated in art and met in a figure drawing class. A high value was placed on visual expression in their household, with Susan's mother, Miriam Garrett, expressing her own visual creativity primarily through the beautiful sewing she did for herself and her daughters. It was Miriam who first taught Susan to appreciate well-made buttons, admonishing her that "buttons always make the outfit."

It wasn't until 1985 that Susan found a way to bring her love of art and history together in one new, unique product. In the past two decades, Grandmother's Buttons has grown into a nationally distributed jewelry company. New to the company is Scrapbook Jewelry: Charmsakes, sterling bracelets hung with porcelain charms that customers can have imprinted with their own family's photographs. Both Scrapbook Jewelry and antique button pieces can be ordered on the company's web site, www.grandmothersbuttons.com. In 1989, Susan's husband, Donny, joined Grandmother's Buttons full time as its business manager. In 1995 they opened a flagship retail store in St. Francisville's 1905 bank building, complete with a button museum in the old bank vault. Both are highly committed to working with local civic organizations to see that their idyllic small town keeps much of the rural ambiance for which it is treasured. They have two children, Anna and Ben, who daily lend their own support to the business. And Miriam Garrett, now in her 80s, visits regularly and relishes the company's growth.

Below: Susan, her mother Miriam, and daughter Anna enjoy each other's company at Grandmother's Buttons.

CREDITS

A Red Lips 4 Courage Book

Eileen Cannon Paulin,
Jayne Cosh, Rebecca Ittner,
Catherine Risling

8502 E. Chapman Ave.,303
Orange, CA 92869
www.redlips4courage.com

Book Editor
Rebecca Ittner

Copy Editor
Catherine Risling

Graphic Design
Kehoe + Kehoe Design
Burlington, VT

Stylist
Rebecca Ittner

Photography
Zac Williams

Contributing Photographer
Terri Fensel
www.terrifensel.com
Page 140

CONTRIBUTORS

About Celeste Layrisson

Celeste Layrisson is a mother of four grown sons. She completed her college degree and MBA while a stay-at-home mother. She and a partner had an antiques shop in her small town, Ponchatoula, Louisiana, "America's Antique City," for 10 years. After completing her master's degree, she worked in banking for 3½ years. Soon after starting that job she realized she really didn't like the world of business that much and wanted to bring some creativity back into her life. So, she quit her job and started selling collectibles on eBay.

Aside from the Bakelite Babies, Celeste creates handmade paper notions (greeting cards, folders, and other items) with fine paper, buttons, textiles, and other materials.

About Anna Macedo

"Every bead is a prayer." That's what Sparky Shooting Star, Anna Macedo's Native American friend, said as she taught her the peyote stitch in 1998. From then on, Anna has been a bead worshipper extraordinaire. Her first four pieces were accepted at Embellishments, an international competition, and now her work is in private collections in four countries.

Anna's graphic design work has appeared in *Architectural Digest*, *The Dover Book of American Trademarks*, *Final Proof*, and *Print Magazine's Regional Design Annual*. Her illustrations for baby goods and fabric prints can be seen in retail stores throughout the United States.

Anna dwells happily with her dog, Satchel, and her cat, Ed Nightly, in a sunny pink house on a tree-lined street, deep in mysterious Louisiana.

You can view Anna Macedo's fanciful artworks, including her original greeting cards and posters, at www.annamacedo.com.

About Joanna McLemore

Joanna McLemore is a full-time student at Baton Rouge Community College who juggles her time between school; designing and making jewelry for Grandmother's Buttons; working as a part-time barista; teaching piano; and dabbling in paint, collage, and custom jewelry. Twilight, the deeps of the ocean, and the intricate forms found in interweaving branches are some of her inspirations.

About Nancy Rothschild

Nancy Rothschild lives in St. Francisville, Louisiana with her husband and three children. She taught art in elementary and secondary schools for 17 years, all the while creating her own sculptural clay pieces for sale to galleries and collectors. Several years ago, she resumed an old interest in beaded jewelry design and for a period of time designed jewelry for Grandmother's Buttons.

OTHER CONTRIBUTORS

Grandmother's Buttons is essentially a close-knit family of creative people, so no project like this could have been done without significant contributions from many on our staff. Susan Lindsay, our resourceful and talented store display artist, contributed her artistic skills and crocheting prowess to the interpretation of two traditional crocheted button jewelry patterns. This is especially pleasing to me, since Susan was the first person to whom

I sold button jewelry 20 years ago. She was at the time managing another local gift shop, and I came in, green as could be, with an actual shoe box full of button earrings. Her enthusiastic reception to my early wares had, and still has, great meaning to me.

Katie Ravencraft pitched in by designing several of the bead and button earrings shown to complement the necklaces and bracelets. Katie, a sophmore in Fashion Merchandising at Louisiana State University, also creates and sells her own beaded jewelry.

I could not end without thanking our incredible Grandmother's Buttons full-time staff: production manager Melissa Roark; production workers Cynthia Standridge and Corda Walker; administrative assistant Kelly Walker; shipping manager Laura Waltman; and store manager Tamie Miller. And of course, my ever-patient partner in business and life, Donny Davis.

WHERE TO FIND IT

Bead Works
www.beadworks.com

Fire Mountain Gems
www.firemountaingems.com

Ornamental Resources
www.ornabead.com

Rings & Things
www.rings-things.com

Rio Grande
www.riogrande.com

Shipwreck Beads
www.shipwreckbeads.com

York Beads
www.yorkbeads.com

Location

Thank you to Mary Thompson for so generously hosting our long days of photo shoots at her lovely plantation home. Catalpa Plantation is a late-Victorian cottage in St. Francisville, Louisiana, and is known for the beautiful gardens that surround it. The oak trees lining the grounds were planted in 1814, and are still a wonder to drive through.

INDEX

A

Abalone & Stick Pearl Earrings 78-81

Abalone Button & Stick Pearl Bracelet 78-81

Adapting a pin design 38

Adding buckle drops 124

Anna Macedo 140

Anna's Folly Necklace 132-135

Anniversary Bracelet 108-111

Antique Mother-of-Pearl Buttons 76-91

Antique Porcelain & China Buttons 92-105

B

Back to School 1957 Necklace 128-131

Bakelite & Celluloid Buttons 116-139

Bakelite & Coral Earrings 122-125

Bakelite & Coral Necklace 122-125

Bakelite Babies 118-119

Bakelite Ball Earrings 120-121

Bakelite Button Elastic Bracelet 120-121

Bead caps 19

Beaded Calico Button Bracelet 94-97

Beaded Calico Button Earrings 94-97

Brass & Cut Steel Filigree Button Earrings 28-31

Brass & Cut Steel Filigree Button Necklace 28-31

Bunches of Brass Buttons Bracelet 32-35

Bunches of Brass Buttons Earrings 32-35

Button history 12-15

C

Caring for Celluloid Buttons 126

Celeste Layrisson 141

Chain 19

Chain nose pliers 22

Charming details 64

China & Stencil Button Link Necklace 98-99

Choosing pieces for your brooch 104

Collage Brooch 36-39

Collage Earrings 36-39

Collaging bases 19

Concave/round nose pliers 22

Confetti Bracelet 36-39

Confetti Earrings 36-39

Crimp bead 19

Crimping 24

Crimping pliers 22

Crocheted Carved Pearl Necklace 82-83

Crocheted Jet Glass Bracelet 72-75

Cut Steel Button Charm Watch 44-45

D

Designing free-form 38

Disc loop bracelets 19

E

Earring clips 19

Earring posts 20

Elastic cording 20

Etched Victorian Pearl Brooch with Beads 84-87

Etched Victorian Pearl Link Bracelet 84-87

Etched Victorian Pearl Link Earrings 84-87

Eurowires 19

Expandable link bracelet 20

Extender chain 20

Eye pin 20

F

Filigree stampings defined 104

Findings 18

Finishing bracelets or necklaces 25

Fishing Tackle Pearl Button Earrings 88-89

Fishing Tackle Pearl Button Necklace 88-89

French ear wire 20

G

Getting the right look 32

Glass Pearl Bead & Button Medallion Necklace 40-43

Glass Pearl Bead & Button Rosette Earrings 40-43

Gumdrop Bracelet 136-139

H

Head pin 20

Hook and eye closures 21

I

Identifying Celluloid Buttons 126

Identifying the age of a button 30

J

Jet Luster Glass Button Earrings 72-75

Jewelry glue 22

Joanna McLemore 140

Jump ring 21

L

Lobster claw 21

M

Making bead dangle 25

Making loops or eyes 24

Midsummer Midnight Necklace 46-49

Modern Glass Buttons 106-115

N

Nancy Rothschild 141

Natural Stone Donut Charm Bracelet 50-53

Natural Stone Strung Bracelet 54-57

O

Oriental Button & Carnelian Earrings 58-61

Oriental Button & Carnelian Necklace 58-61

Oriental Button Carnelian Bracelet 58-61

P

Pearl Button Earrings 56-57

Pearls, Buttons & Cuff Links Charm Necklace 62-65

Pearls of wisdom 42

Pin back 21

Pin back with bail 21

Poppy Jasper Donut Button Earrings 50-53

Poppy Jasper Donut Pendant 54-57

Positioning earrings 114

R

Reversible Victorian Jet Glass Button Necklace 72-75

Rhinestone Button Clip-on Earrings 108-111

Rhyolite or Turquoise Donut
Earrings 56-57

Ring and toggle 21

S

Scissors 22

Shank disguisers 22

Shoe Button & Vintage Bead
Earrings 108-111

Stacked Celluloid Button
Brooches 126-127

Stacked Pearl & Victorian
Metal Brooches 90-91

Stacked Porcelain Button
Brooches 104-105

Stampings 21

Stencil Button Bracelet 100-103

Stencil Button Earrings 98-99

Stick Pearl Brooch 78-81

Strand spacer 21

Strong-hold glue 22

Surgeon's knot 25

Susan Davis 140

T

The allure of enamel buttons 90

The cost of Bakelite 122

Tools 22

Toothpicks 22

Treasure Necklace 66-69

Turning watches into lockets 64

V

Victorian Jet Glass Buttons
70-75

Victorian Metal Buttons 26-69

W

Watch face 22

West German Glass Button
Bracelet 112-115

West German Glass Button
Earrings 112-115

Wire cutters 22

Wire wrapping two- or four-
hole button to make dangle
or chain link 25

BIBLIOGRAPHY

About Buttons: A Collectors Guide, 150 A.D. to the Present by Peggy Ann Osborne, Schiffer Publishing, Ltd., Atglen, PA ©1994

Antique and Collectible Buttons by Debra J. Wisniewski, Collector Books, Paducah, KY ©1997

The Big Book of Buttons by Elizabeth Hughes and Marion Lester, New Leaf Publishers, Sedgwick, ME ©1991

Buttons by Diana Epstein and Millicent Safro, Harry Abrams, New York, NY ©1991

The Button Book by Diana Epstein, Running Press, Philadelphia & London ©1996

The Collector's Encyclopedia of Buttons by Sally Luscomb, Crown Publishers, Inc., New York, NY, ©1967. Reprinted by Schiffer Publishing Ltd., Atglen, PA ©1992 & ©1997

Fun Buttons by Peggy Ann Osborne, Schiffer Publishing Ltd., Atglen, PA ©1994

METRIC EQUIVALENCY CHARTS

inches to millimeters and centimeters
mm-millimeters cm-centimeters

inches	mm	cm	inches	cm	inches	cm
⅛	3	0.3	9	22.9	30	76.2
¼	6	0.6	10	25.4	31	78.7
½	13	1.3	12	30.5	33	83.8
⅝	16	1.6	13	33.0	34	86.4
¾	19	1.9	14	35.6	35	88.9
⅞	22	2.2	15	38.1	36	91.4
1	25	2.5	16	40.6	37	94.0
1¼	32	3.2	17	43.2	38	96.5
1½	38	3.8	18	45.7	39	99.1
1¾	44	4.4	19	48.3	40	101.6
2	51	5.1	20	50.8	41	104.1
2½	64	6.4	21	53.3	42	106.7
3	76	7.6	22	55.9	43	109.2
3½	89	8.9	23	58.4	44	111.8
4	102	10.2	24	61.0	45	114.3
4½	114	11.4	25	63.5	46	116.8
5	127	12.7	26	66.0	47	119.4
6	152	15.2	27	68.6	48	121.9
7	178	17.8	28	71.1	49	124.5
8	203	20.3	29	73.7	50	127.0

yards to meters

yards	meters	yards	meters	yards	meters	yards	meters	yards	meters
⅛	0.11	2⅛	1.94	4⅛	3.77	6⅛	5.60	8⅛	7.43
¼	0.23	2¼	2.06	4¼	3.89	6¼	5.72	8¼	7.54
⅜	0.34	2⅜	2.17	4⅜	4.00	6⅜	5.83	8⅜	7.66
½	0.46	2½	2.29	4½	4.11	6½	5.94	8½	7.77
⅝	0.57	2⅝	2.40	4⅝	4.23	6⅝	6.06	8⅝	7.89
¾	0.69	2¾	2.51	4¾	4.34	6¾	6.17	8¾	8.00
⅞	0.80	2⅞	2.63	4⅞	4.46	6⅞	6.29	8⅞	8.12
1	0.91	3	2.74	5	4.57	7	6.40	9	8.23
1⅛	1.03	3⅛	2.86	5⅛	4.69	7⅛	6.52	9⅛	8.34
1¼	1.14	3¼	2.97	5¼	4.80	7¼	6.63	9¼	8.46
1⅜	1.26	3⅜	3.09	5⅜	4.91	7⅜	6.74	9⅜	8.57
1½	1.37	3½	3.20	5½	5.03	7½	6.86	9½	8.69
1⅝	1.49	3⅝	3.31	5⅝	5.14	7⅝	6.97	9⅝	8.80
1¾	1.60	3¾	3.43	5¾	5.26	7¾	7.09	9¾	8.92
1⅞	1.71	3⅞	3.54	5⅞	5.37	7⅞	7.20	9⅞	9.03
2	1.83	4	3.66	6	5.49	8	7.32	10	9.14

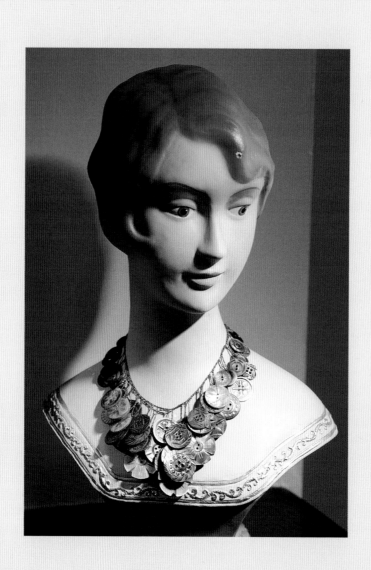